Let's do a Musical

PETER A. SPENCER

Let's do a Musical

Studio Vista London

For my mother and father

The author is grateful to the many people who have helped in the compilation of this book. In particular, acknowledgement is made to the following: Sydney Lockerman and Alan Legget of the Wood Green Operatic Society; Nellie Lindsey of the Forest Operatic Society; John Hughes and F. Leslie Cowham of the National Operatic and Dramatic Association; Bob Bevan of Charles Fox Ltd; Alfred Rogers of W. and G. Foyle Ltd; L. Jordan of Strand Electric and Engineering Company Ltd; George Hoare, Manager, Theatre Royal, Drury Lane; Tom Arnold Ltd; Jack Hylton Ltd; The Wood Green Operatic Society for permission to reproduce the rules of the society; and Miss Avril Hunt and Eric Hiscock without whom this book would never have been written. The extract from *Pink Champagne* is reprinted by kind permission of Eric Maschwitz, Bernard Grun and the publishers of *Pink Champagne*—Samuel French Ltd.

Published in Great Britain 1968 by Studio Vista Limited
Blue Star House, Highgate Hill, London N19
Distributed in Canada by General Publishing Co. Limited
30 Lesmill Road, Don Mills, Toronto, Ontario
Set in 11/12 point Garamond
Made and printed in Great Britain by
W. S. Cowell Limited at the Butter Market, Ipswich

SBN 289 27669 1

Contents

Foreword

The general standard of amateur stage presentations has risen noticeably over recent years. Most amateur societies today attract their audiences primarily by virtue of the quality of the shows they put on. There is still room for improvement, but the vast majority of societies are concerned that each member of the audience receives entertainment value commensurate with the price charged for the seat. As overall production costs continue to rise, so the society has to aim for bigger box office returns in order to stay modestly solvent. This means that seat prices have to be put up and – bearing in mind the counter-attractions offered by television, cinema and (in many areas) the professional theatre – the amateur knows his audience will not come out of charity. They come to see a show they like, presented and performed sufficiently well to make their journey and their visit worthwhile.

More and more societies are realising that one of the most important factors leading to their ultimate success is the engaging of a competent, artistic and conscientious producer. The right choice here can mean wise help in show selection (bearing in mind the talents and capabilities of the society's members), due and unbiased care in casting, strong guidance and training during rehearsals, co-ordination of the various ancillary functions (scenery, costumes, lighting, make-up, staging and the like). All this leads to a public performance when each member is impelled to give of his (or her) very best, with enthusiasm and confidence . . . for the greatest delight and entertainment of the audience.

The vital necessity of choosing and engaging the best available producer cannot be overstressed. It is no exaggeration to say that a good producer enables a moderate society to put on a splendid show, while an inadequate producer can make a strong society appear weak.

The author of this book has been a source of inspiration to many societies over the years. He brings an artistic and imaginative consideration to bear on each production: he coaches whilst producing and he possesses the skill that commands attention. He brings the professional approach to the amateur theatre that is so essential for the amateur's success and continuing advancement. In the pages that follow Peter Spencer is preaching what he practises and, if the study of this book helps to increase the number of competent producers available within the amateur movement, then it will have achieved its laudable objective.

F. Leslie Cowham, London Councillor,
National Operatic and Dramatic Association

Overture

In the February 1966 issue of the *Noda Bulletin*, the official magazine of the *National Operatic and Dramatic Association*, there were over 600 musicals listed for presentation by amateurs in Great Britain in the spring. Since most operatic societies present two musicals in the year, this gives a rough count of 1,200 productions. This figure does not take into account all the other companies who are not members of Noda. Therefore it would not be an exaggeration to say that in any one year there are over 2,000 productions of musical shows performed by amateurs in Great Britain – and all of these need the services of a producer!

What is a producer? The *Oxford Dictionary* relegates the title to the addendum and merely states '. . . *person generally responsible for the production of a film or play*'. *The Oxford Companion to the Theatre* is rather more forthcoming. It starts: '*In England the man responsible for the general interpretation of the play, and for the conduct of rehearsals, during which he guides and advises the actors, welding them into a corporate body. He has no responsibility for the financial or business side of the production, but only for its artistic and dramatic integration.*' The final paragraph is particularly interesting . . . '*It has also been said that the ideal producer must be an actor, an artist, an architect, an electrician, an expert in geography, history, costume, accessories and scenery, and have a thorough understanding of human nature – the last trait being the most essential.*'

In his book – *Producing Plays* – C. B. Purdom writes of the producer as '. . . *one whose business it is to prepare the play for performance, to rehearse the players, and to put the play on the stage. He directs its interpretation from start to finish by controlling the players, the scenery, lighting, costumes and the use of the stage.*'

The same high standards are required of a producer of opera, operetta or musical comedy, with the additional qualification of a knowledge of music and choreography. How can the would-be amateur producer start to acquire this, for, make no mistake, once one takes up production one never stops learning – there are always new techniques to master, fresh fields to conquer.

Schools exist where one can take a course in play production and Noda runs an annual summer school for the benefit of its members. But there is no better way to acquire the knowledge and experience than by actually undertaking a job or a role in as many varied productions as possible. In this way one can gain an insight into the requirements of a producer at other people's expense. Be prepared to undertake stage management, help with scene painting, try your skill at making stage properties, in fact do any task that will help to build up the store of knowledge and experience from which you will eventually need to draw.

In addition, try to see as many productions, both professional and amateur, as your purse will allow. If possible cultivate an acquaintance with a professional company so that you may be allowed to sit-in at rehearsals or visit backstage. Note all that you see and hear: how the producer tackles a rehearsal; how the sets are designed; how the lighting effects are managed and study the various techniques employed by the actors.

Use your eyes constantly, taking note of such everyday things as the behaviour of individuals in a busy street, a particularly effective shop-window display, the techniques employed in the best films, for one day you may need to use these experiences to help a cast of your own.

When I started to write this book, I thought back to my first production and recalled those points on which I needed guidance. I have tried to cover them all, so far as I can, in the chapters that follow. They are, naturally, one person's ideas on the way to tackle a musical and should be read in conjunction with the books mentioned in the bibliography, and in the light of your own experience.

In conclusion, I must confess that I cannot tell you how to become a producer. This is largely a question of luck and being in the right place at the right time. You can only prepare yourself for the time when an offer comes your way and this book is intended to assist you, in some small measure, with your endeavours.

1 The operatic society

'*. . . the song is you!*'
ROBERT AND ELIZABETH

INTRODUCTION

Musicals are fun, both for the actors and the producer. Combining singing, acting and dancing, they create a colourful, romantic world to which players and audience alike can escape for a few hours and therein lies their popular appeal. To the production team they present a challenge which will exert their talents and imagination to the full.

In the following chapters I shall attempt to trace the growth of a production from its inception to the finished performance, as seen through the eyes of the producer. Casting, rehearsals, scenery, lighting, stage management and the actual presentation will be discussed as well as ways of avoiding the more common pitfalls.

To do this, I must assume that you, the reader, have a love for the theatre in general and some practical experience of the amateur theatre in particular. Whether the latter is gained with a musical company is not important, although it is an asset to have a basic knowledge and appreciation of music since at least half of your production will be involved with this aspect.

Nowadays, the term producer is synonymous with director in the theatre (as opposed to the cinema) and in this book I shall refer only to the producer. To produce one needs a company and in the majority of cases it is the company that chooses its producer. One will be approached and asked to undertake the production of a specified show. The choice of show is generally decided by the company before a producer is appointed, and it is only in exceptional circumstances that you will be given the opportunity to select a show.

A COMPANY OF YOUR OWN

This may tempt you to decide to form your own company in order to produce shows of your own choosing, but be warned against such a move. Musicals are costly to mount, they require a large body of varied talents and even a light show like *The Boy Friend* can run away with several hundred pounds.

I once became involved in the founding of a now flourishing group in Toronto. A lot of private financial backing was necessary merely to recruit a company. The cost of advertising preliminary auditions, hire of audition rooms and scores, postage and telephone calls, soon mounted up before rehearsals had even started. Even working on a shoe-string, supplying our own costumes and making the scenery, the first modest production of *Finian's Rainbow*, played in a simple standing set, cost around £750 resulting in a loss of £300.

The company managed to recoup their losses with subsequent productions and is now a thriving concern. I recount this experience here to show how vital it is to be aware of the financial dangers involved in forming a new group.

THE ESTABLISHED COMPANY

Better therefore to make one's debut with an established amateur operatic society. Many of these groups exist, not only in the United Kingdom, but, literally, in all corners of the globe, as a glance at any *Noda Bulletin* will prove. In the main, they are firmly established on a sound economic basis, with a long and continuous list of productions over the years. They will fall broadly into one of two groups. There are those attached or affiliated in some way to localized groups or large organizations. These will include the school and church societies as well as the companies formed of employees of large stores, business concerns, factories and youth organizations. Very often they are sponsored by and receive financial support from their parent body, and enjoy the advantages of free or cheap rehearsal and staging facilities. Then there are the independent groups who are entirely self-supporting who often have a continual struggle to make ends meet and, indeed, to keep alive. Today, luckily, most of these companies are eligible for some form of assistance from their local Arts Council and there is a growing tendency for local authorities to encourage and support the 'live theatre' in their locality.

NODA

The hard core of amateur operatic societies are affiliated to the National Operatic and Dramatic Association, an organization established in 1899. It is the only organization of its kind in the world, and its energies are devoted to the amateur musical and dramatic stage in both hemispheres. Membership is available to both companies and individuals and full details can be obtained by writing to the secretary at Noda's head office at 1 Crestfield Street, London, WC1.

The many benefits that membership of Noda confers, and which are of particular interest to the producer, include the free use of their extensive library of over 30,000 volumes. These cover every aspect of production, including libretti and vocal and orchestral scores, as well as a set of comprehensive synopses of over 100 operas and musical comedies. In addition Noda will give free legal advice; arrange substitute players in an emergency; arrange insurance schemes for a production at advantageous premiums and frequently find productions for suitable producers. A free periodical, *Noda Bulletin*, is issued to all members and this gives full details of current and forthcoming amateur productions, new releases and numerous articles on all aspects of amateur theatre. The producer of amateur musicals would be well advised to become a member early in his career.

Whilst not involved in the politics of the company, it is desirable that the producer should know something about the organization and management of an amateur operatic society. By and large, their constitution and rules will be based on the model suggested by Noda. The Wood Green Operatic Society is one such company and I am indebted to their general management committee for allowing me to quote at length from their rules, which will be found in the appendix, p. 108.

The day-to-day running of the society is in the hands of the general management committee which is comprised of the officers together with other elected members of the society.

The officers with whom the producer will chiefly have dealings are the secretary, business manager and publicity manager and of these, the secretary will be his main link with the management committee.

The secretary will see that rehearsal rooms are booked, that rehearsal accompanists are engaged and ensure that the company are made aware of the rehearsal calls. He will also organize the auditors, obtain the scores and libretti, and often issue the contracts for hire of scenery, costumes, lighting equipment and so on. He should also be cognisant of the various legal aspects of the production, and attend to the formalities which evolve from the use of children in a production, as well as with insurance and copyright questions. Many of these tasks can be delegated and very often the business manager will attend to all aspects relating to the actual production in hand. However, all records should be kept by the secretary and it is to him, initially, that the producer should turn for advice or assistance on policy matter.

Although I firmly believe that the producer should make himself personally responsible for such matters as the selection of scenery, furniture, properties and costumes and where possible see the actual articles he intends to use, he should always have his selection officially confirmed by either the secretary or the business manager on behalf of the company.

It is advisable for the producer to liaise with the publicity manager on the question of advertising so that the company's publicity reflects the style of the production that he has in mind. Questions of billing credits and synopsis of scenes should be discussed as the producer's ideas may often vary from the printed acting editions. The publicity manager will often be responsible for the front of house decoration and photographs (see chapter 10).

The production team   The production team itself will be fully discussed in ensuing chapters but its composition is worth noting here. Apart from the producer, it will include some or all of the following:

>Musical director · Chorus master · Choreographer or dancing mistress · Stage manager · Assistant stage manager · Company electrician · Stage carpenter · Art director · Property master · Wardrobe mistress · Accompanist(s) · Prompter · Call boy(s) or girl(s) · Make-up artist · Sound and effects engineer

With the possible exception of the producer, musical director and choreographer, the members of the production team will usually be drawn from the society. Some of the duties listed above may be combined: for example, the musical director will very often also act as chorus master while the stage manager may attend to the devising and recording of sound effects.

The acting members   The members of the company will fall broadly into four groups: principals, chorus, dancers and extras. In most cases the principal players will have graduated from the chorus, although in certain cases, outsiders may be invited to play principal roles. Dancers are selected for their ability but may also be choristers while, as their name suggests, extras are recruited from any available source to help swell the numbers or undertake walk-on parts when it is undesirable to deplete the vocal strength by allocating the part to a chorister. In addition there will be a team of backstage and front-of-house helpers. These are members whose interest lies in the technical and management aspects of the production and who have no desire to 'tread the boards'.

The initial readings and production conference Having been appointed producer, the first task is to read the show and become acquainted with the score. Here one should merely aim for a general understanding of the piece. If you have ever painted in oils, this stage is comparable to the initial blocking-in of a canvas. One seeks an overall conception and there is no reference to detail.

When a musical is a result of an adaptation of a play or book, reference to the original work will yield useful information. Well-known examples would include *Pygmalion* for the producer of *My Fair Lady* or the *Surtees* stories for the producer of *Jorrocks*. While among the lesser known one may cite *Liliom* for *Carousel* or *Green Grow the Lilacs* for *Oklahoma*.

The musical director, choreographer and stage manager should, at the same time, be studying the show from their own particular viewpoints. Many readings and a lot of mental exertion will be necessary before one progresses to the first production conference. At this meeting, the four people who will be chiefly concerned with the production will pool their ideas and discuss at length the way in which the show will be staged.

This in no way reduces the producer's influence on the finished work, but, unlike his counterpart in the legitimate theatre, the producer of musicals is one of a team. True, he is the guiding force, and he will ultimately make all the decisions, but, ideally, it is from a team effort that the best production will result.

Whatever definite ideas the producer may have regarding the interpretation of the show, he must consider the needs of both the choreographer and musical director. When, for example, the show requires the chorus to be divided into two separate sets of characters, he may have to arrange for certain principals who are not normally required for a specific vocal number, to bolster the vocal strength. Again, he must consider the stage area available for the choreographer and when a dance takes place on a crowded stage, place his chorus accordingly. The stage manager will be able to advise on the practicability or otherwise of ideas raised and the producer should give full consideration to his points.

In addition to the technical considerations, the team will have a variety of ideas on the general conception of the show. If the production under discussion is a time-worn Savoy opera, consideration should be given as to whether it should be re-staged or played traditionally. It was from such an exchange of ideas that my up-dated Carnaby Street send-up of *Patience* was born.

The constant interchange of ideas should be encouraged at this meeting and the resultant ideas crystallized into an overall basic interpretation that includes all the departments of acting, singing, dancing and staging. Beware, however, of change for the sake of change. Every idea propounded should be argued out and if the idea is not logically viable, it should be discounted. The result of these discussions will be a general idea of the finished product. Details will be worked out later, but the producer can now move on to his next and all-important task – the preparation of his prompt book – this deserves a chapter to itself.

2 The producer's script

'You hold yourself like this . . .'
PATIENCE

INTRODUCTION

Musical comedies, or musicals as they are more generally termed today, owe their origins to a fusion of burlesque and light opera which took place towards the end of the last century. They were basically a series of musical items loosely connected by a basic story-line but, whilst the libretto had a plot (albeit a weak one!) the musical items rarely had any relation to it or to the characters of the piece. Many a song already made popular by the leading artiste, was interpolated into the production with little or no regard being paid to its aptness. But the audiences of the time expected this and no one complained. Not until the advent of *Oklahoma!* did story and music become closely allied and the plot carry through both the dialogue and musical items. This marriage of all the aspects of a musical continued to develop, through the Rodgers and Hammerstein shows, to the present day and such current successes as *Fiddler on the Roof*. What the future holds one can only surmise, but I have heard rumours of a new musical being devised by Gower Champion, of *Hello Dolly* fame, called *I do, I do!* It will have a total cast of two!

EDITING THE BOOK

The older, lesser-known shows usually require revitalizing and yet, with a new, modern libretto, they would no longer be unknown! The bubbling scores of Offenbach have been given new life with their new up-to-date translations and are now being played regularly by the Sadler's Wells Opera Company, and many librettists are turning their attentions to antique musicals, giving them a face lift, and a new lease of life.

Apart from editing the libretto, the amateur producer will often have to accept that there are no complete sets of band parts available, no official sets of scenery, or costumes, and vocal scores and libretti are out of print. Faced with these problems, it is small wonder that most companies stick to the familiar repertoire of musicals; yet there is a wealth of material available to the producer and company with the enthusiasm to tackle a show from scratch.

It is generally advisable to keep the playing time of any musical to about two and a half hours, including any intervals. Indeed, if one is in the habit of playing two houses – late matinee and evening performance – on Saturdays, the production must be tailored to these limits.

The Gilbert and Sullivan operas fall easily into this time span, especially if the traditional encores are sensibly pruned, but both the modern musical and the period extravaganza run nearer to three hours. Few productions will fail to benefit from judicious pruning when performed by amateurs, but here we come up against the law of copyright.

In law, the words and music are the property of the copyright holders. They may not be cut or altered without permission, but the owners are generally most understanding and ready to help the amateur and I have never been refused permission to make such amendments as I found necessary for technical or physical reasons. Indeed, some go so far as to indicate cuts and alterations in their printed libretti and scores. The Weinberger version of *The Gipsy Baron* is a case in point.

What should be cut? There can be no general answer for every production will have its particular problems. Apart from keeping the performance to a reasonable length, one must also consider the editing of lines which cease to have their original meaning or which evoke the wrong audience response. Musical items, too, can often be pruned with advantage. To cite an example, the celebrated Totem Dance in *Rose Marie* is plotted in the acting edition to run to nine choruses, plus calls! (There is an amusing footnote to the choreographer suggesting that some dancers be kept as standbyes, since the number is somewhat strenuous. One can picture the dancing mistress standing in the wings with a megaphone calling 'Come in number six, your time's up!') When originally played at Drury Lane, with a large stage company and stage facilities, this number was a show-stopper and not considered unduly long, but if played in full at the average community theatre by amateur dancers it may over-extend the goodwill of an audience. I also deplore the habit, now fortunately lapsing, of giving all the traditional encores in the Savoy operas, whether or not the audience response warrants them. All encores should be planned and rehearsed but they should only be given if demanded by the applause. In general I am a firm believer in the old adage: 'Always leave them wanting more'.

Cuts or alterations should only be made after a great deal of thought, and in consultation with the musical director and the choreographer when they affect the music or the dancing. They should be made before the first read-through since this avoids disappointment among your cast who may otherwise feel that their parts are being unreasonably shortened. If necessary, explain to them why you have made the cuts and how these will benefit the show as a whole.

THE PROMPT BOOK

The preparation of the prompt book is probably the most arduous chore that a producer has to undertake. Every production needs one, though there may be wide differences of opinion about what it should contain. I consider that the prompt book should be the producer's and stage manager's *vade-mecum*. In it should be found all the actor's entrances and exits, all the moves and bits of business, the cuts, pauses, notes on inflections, pace, speech rhythms, together with music cues, lighting, effects and curtain cues. In short, it should contain all the information that is needed to show how the piece will be staged and certainly in the early stages of directorship I suggest that as much detail as possible be annotated.

In order to get this information written down in a neat and accessible form, both the libretto and the vocal score should be interleaved with blank sheets of paper. This can be done in several ways, but I strongly recommend that you seek out a bookbinder to interleave your copies and bind them with a stiff cover. Several will do this simple operation using what is known in the trade as 'perfect binding' which allows the volumes to open flat at any page. The cost of this service, usually around thirty shillings, is fully justified since the libretto and score will undergo severe handling during the weeks of preparation and rehearsal.

The most important information in the prompt book is the blocking. Blocking is, in essence, deciding how a scene shall be played; how, why and where the actors move in the scene, and these moves are marked in the prompt book together with any notes on inflection, pace, business and so on.

When to block In the straight theatre, as opposed to musicals, there is a great deal of argument about when blocking should be undertaken. Some producers will plan every detail in advance of rehearsals, and will appear at the first staging rehearsal with the entire production worked out. Others will not dream of attempting to block the show until their first meeting with the actors. There are pros and cons for these and other methods, and these are discussed at some length by Curtis Canfield in his admirable book, *The Craft of Play Directing*. He, like myself, comes down finally in favour of pre-rehearsal blocking.

Dolman, in *The Art of Acting*, suggests that there are three reasons for rehearsing: experiment; teaching the text and its meaning; perfecting and polishing. Pre-rehearsal blocking gives a basic idea from which to experiment and develop, for no sensible producer will regard his initial blocking as sacrosanct. He will most certainly block in rehearsals as well, adjusting, correcting and refining his original conception. Furthermore, a producer who comes to his first staging rehearsal with the details of his production firmly established in his mind, will imbue his cast with confidence in his ability to direct them.

French scenes   When I start blocking, I first go through the libretto and underline all the directions and stage business in red ink. I note any cuts or alterations at the same time, and strike any vocal items or dialogue over music out of the libretto, making a cross-reference to the appropriate page in the vocal score.

I then consider the libretto in terms of 'French scenes'. Curtis Canfield defines these as '. . . *textual segments based on a stabilized number of characters present on the stage at the same time*'. In a musical these are usually easily delineated by the musical items. For example, Act 1 scene 1 of *The Wizard of Oz* can be broken down into four French scenes as follows:

1 From curtain rise to Dorothy's entrance
2 Dialogue between Dorothy and Aunt Em, ending with Aunt Em's exit
3 Dorothy's song and general entrance of chorus
4 Entrance of Uncle Henry after song to end of the scene

These scenes are then plotted, bearing in mind their relation to the show as a whole. This will of necessity involve a great deal of experiment. One may use counters, golf tees or chessmen to represent the individual characters and manœuvre them on a scale drawing of the set. The more ambitious producer may prepare a scale model of his sets, on which to plan out his production; others may find rough sketches, similar to a film or television story board will serve the experimental stage. Symbols often assist in the task. These are the ones that I use, but others, equally effective, will no doubt suggest themselves to you (fig. 1).

FIG 1   Some suggested symbols for use in the producer's script

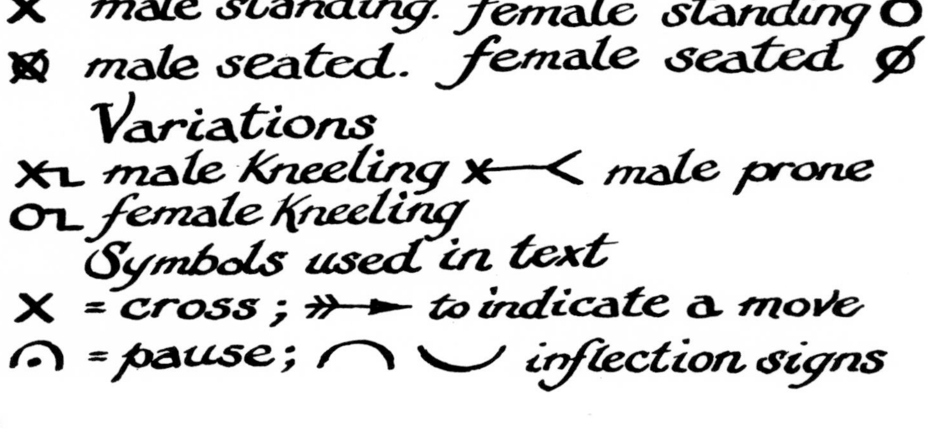

X *male standing. female standing* **O**

⊠ *male seated. female seated* **ø**

Variations

X⌐ *male kneeling* **x—<** *male prone*

O⌐ *female kneeling*

Symbols used in text

X = *cross ; ⇻► to indicate a move*

⊙ = *pause ;* ⌢ ⌣ *inflection signs*

Some basic rules should be remembered:

1 Generally speaking, actors should only move on their own lines
2 An actor speaking should cross downstage of another
3 A moving actor attracts the attention provided he contrasts others who are static
4 Wherever possible, lines should be spoken within the confines of the proscenium arch. As soon as an actor addresses his lines above the stage opening, the carrying power of his voice will drop by as much as sixty per cent and he will have to lift his voice to compensate for this loss
5 No move should be made without a purpose. Among the many reasons for a move may be listed: practicality, emphasis, emotion, proportion or balance, character relationships
6 Wherever possible, an actor leaving a scene should be placed near enough to his exit to enable him to give his line and make a clean exit

An example of blocking principal moves Let us now take a short sequence from *Pink Champagne* and block it together. Here is the scene as it appears on pages 17 and 18 in *French's Acting Edition*:

ROSALINDA   (*To herself*) Poor Gabriel! I must say he shows courage – he's going to prison with his head held high. I love him for that. (*With a change of mood*) No, I *don't* love him, I *detest* him! Whatever happens, I'll *never* forgive him for last night! (*With resolution she moves up* R *to windows, and turns up the lamp. Then she crosses* L *to the console table and waits*)
Off stage there is a great noise as Alfred scales the balcony. The music fades out
(*Running to the window.*) Ssh!

Alfred appears at balcony.

ALFRED   (*Fulsomely*) My beloved!

ROSALINDA   (*Moving* C) Be careful, do – the flower pots!
There is a crash of flower pots off stage. Alfred enters and looks around possessively
(*Reproachfully*) Alfred – my husband!

ALFRED   Why worry about *him*? He's on his way to prison. (*He moves down to* R *of Rosalinda*)

ROSALINDA   You *know* about it?

ALFRED   (*With satisfaction*) Of course. It's in every newspaper and a picture of the Bat! (*He kneels and takes her hand*) How an angel like you could have married such a hooligan!

ROSALINDA   (*Pathetically, mopping her eye with her handkerchief*) He *has* been rather – *unkind*!

ALFRED   (*Rising and crossing* L *to the table.*) Unkind? His behaviour has been monstrous. (*Eyeing the table greedily*) Not *supper*?

ROSALINDA   I thought perhaps a glass of wine . . .

ALFRED   (*Moving to* L *of the sofa*) You think of everything. A dressing-gown – a smoking cap. And to think how nervous I was of being alone with my goddess for the first time . . .! (*He removes his jacket*) I never expected to be made at home like this!

ROSALINDA	(*Astonished*) Whatever are you doing?
ALFRED	What seems the most natural thing in the world. I'm taking over the duties of that profligate! (*He puts on the dressing-gown*)
ROSALINDA	His d-d-duties . . .?
ALFRED	You'll be surprised how naturally I slip into them!
ROSALINDA	(*With raised eyebrows*) Surprised is hardly the word!
ALFRED	(*Putting on the smoking cap*) Now what about a little supper, darling wife? (*He moves to the chair above the table L and sits*)
ROSALINDA	(*Doubtfully*) Darling *wife*?
ALFRED	(*Inspecting the tray*) Foie gras – a cold capon – and a bottle of pink champagne. Delicious! (*He picks up the champagne bottle*) I have to be rather particular what I eat.
ROSALINDA	(*Nettled*) Oh, you *do*, do you?
ALFRED	My voice, you know. (*He sings a scale*) Now, as for breakfast . . .
ROSALINDA	(*Horrified*) Breakfast?
ALFRED	Love gives one the appetite of a god. All the same I must be careful. Just some lightly boiled eggs – a dish of sweetbreads – a little fish – a slice of ham – a toasted roll or two . . . (*He unfastens the champagne bottle*)
ROSALINDA	(*Cutting in*) Don't imagine that you're going to breakfast *here*!
ALFRED	You would rather go out, my love?
ROSALINDA	(*Sweeping agitatedly upstage and then down*) You'll be going out – and long before breakfast, too! Do you want to destroy my reputation entirely?
ALFRED	(*Aside, opening the bottle*) I can see that I have been a little impetuous. I should have let things take their course. (*Aloud*) Do not worry, Rosalinda mine. (*He rises and, moving to R of the table, pours out two glasses of pink champagne*) The night is still young, let us live for the moment, let us say that I am here just to take a glass of wine with you and *sing*?
ROSALINDA	No, no, not *that*!
ALFRED	(*Petulantly*) Not sing? But you used to like my voice?
ROSALINDA	Unfortunately I liked it too much, but tonight . . .
ALFRED	(*Trying to embrace her*) My angel! Come to my arms. This is the moment of which your foolish, adoring Alfred has always dreamed!
ROSALINDA	(*Escaping hastily down R*) I think perhaps you had better *sing* after all!

This scene presents several problems. There is a lot of business with the food, champagne and the glasses, as well as the changing into the dressing-gown. The first problem to resolve is the placing of these important properties, so let us refresh our memory by looking again at the general setting.

The lantern, which is alight, stands on the small table above the French windows UR. The dressing-gown (Eisenstein's) is drooped over the back of the sofa, DC and the smoking cap is on the sofa towards the right end. The supper has already

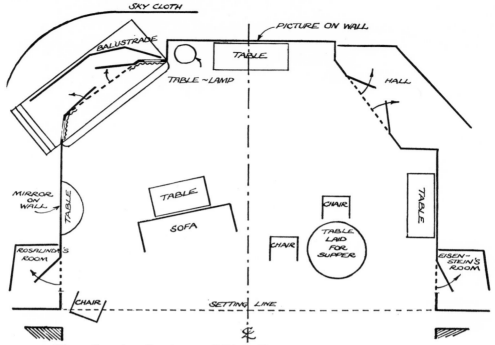

FIG 2 Plan of setting for Act 1 of *Pink Champagne*

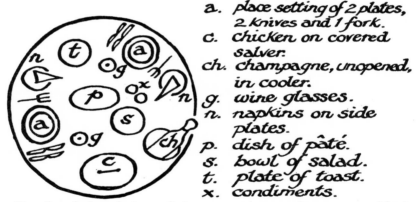

a. place setting of 2 plates, 2 knives and 1 fork.
c. chicken on covered salver.
ch. champagne, unopened, in cooler.
g. wine glasses.
n. napkins on side plates.
p. dish of pâté.
s. bowl of salad.
t. plate of toast.
x. condiments.

FIG 3 Details of the placing of the properties on the supper table in *Pink Champagne*

been laid on the table DLC, and here the placing of the food, cutlery and crockery, is extremely critical if the scene is to play smoothly (fig.3).

The scene starts as Eisenstein leaves, by the double doors UL, supposedly to go to jail. Adele, the maid, leaves at the same time, closing the doors behind her. Rosalinda is DR, gazing after her departing husband (fig. 4).

She turns downstage as she speaks. She is in love with her husband, despite his antics of the previous night and a smile would not be out of place here, and if she holds her hands lightly clasped to her chin, she can make a strong gesture here.

ROSALINDA (*To herself*) Poor Gabriel! I must say he shows courage – he's going to prison with his head held high. I love him for that.

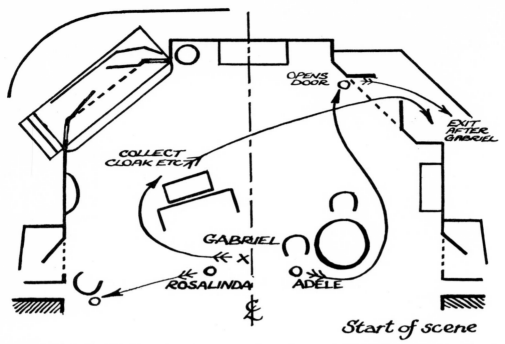

FIG 4 Details of movements in a scene from Act 1 of *Pink Champagne* (see also figs. 5-7)

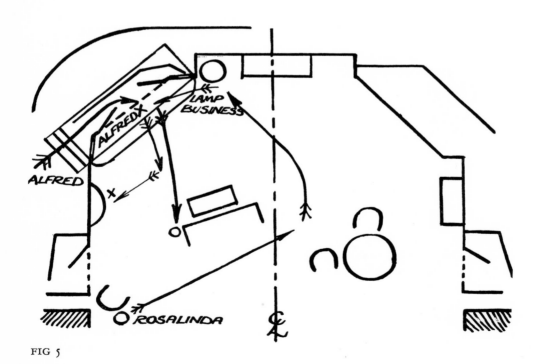

FIG 5

She is in a bad position from which to move to the lamp. She can reinforce her anger with a move – x to table DRC. She looks at the supper for two and this gives her an idea. x above sofa to lamp she waves it as a signal. Replaces it. Suddenly a pang of conscience, she breaks away to R back of sofa (fig. 5).

Alfred is presumably using a creeper to assist his climb to the balcony, and the noise he creates will be of cracking twigs and of his physical exertions. These hardly give rise to a great noise as indicated. Moreover, if Alfred appears on the balcony before giving his line, he will not be seen by a large part of the audience. I decided therefore to bring forward Alfred's 'My beloved!' and let him shout this from off stage. The book now reads:

She must also look down as the room is supposed to be on the first floor! She places a warning finger to her lips.
As he climbs over the balcony Rosalinda can back into the room, and, as Alfred's foot is obviously going straight into her potted geraniums:

Alfred can swear sotto voce 'Damn!'

Having recovered his composure, Alfred makes a very theatrical entrance, arms extended as if to take Rosalinda in an embrace. She turns away to DRC, teasing him.

To underline the fact that Alfred is an egotist and very vain, I altered the suggested move and instead let Alfred go to the mirror on the wall R and admire himself.

Slightly taken aback by his knowledge. Since he is looking away from her he cannot see her concern. Again I have altered the move. Instead of kneeling, he turns to her.

(With a change of mood) No, I *don't* love him, I *detest* him! Whatever happens, I'll *never* forgive him for last night!

(With resolution she moves up R to the windows)

Off stage there is a great noise as Alfred scales the balcony.
ROSALINDA   *(Running to the window)* Ssh!
ALFRED   My Beloved!

Off stage UR there is a great noise as Alfred scales the balcony
ALFRED   (Off UR in loud stage whisper) My beloved!
ROSALINDA   *(Quickly running to window UR and looking off)* Ssh!

Alfred appears on the balcony

ROSALINDA   Be careful, do – the flower pots!
There is a crash of flower pots off stage, UR.

Alfred enters

ROSALINDA   (Reproachfully) Alfred – my husband!

ALFRED   Why worry about *him*? *He's* on his way to prison.

ROSALINDA   You *know* about it?
ALFRED   *(With satisfaction)* Of course. It's in every newspaper, and a picture of the Bat! How an angel like you could have married such a hooligan!

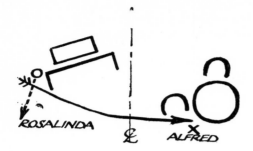

FIG 6

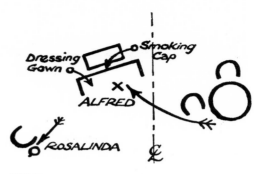

FIG 7

She searches for a suitable word.

Alfred takes her literally x *to her. This brings him in direct line with the supper table. Instead of consoling Rosalinda as she anticipates, he continues his* x *and his speech (fig. 6).*

Rosalinda can show her pique with a break R. *This also serves to clear the sofa for the next sequence. Alfred now turns to reply and in so doing, sees the dressing-gown and smoking cap.*

Here he starts to remove his jacket (fig. 7).

He lays his jacket over the L *end of the sofa. Rosalinda, not knowing what he intends is astonished and* x 2 *to* C.

ROSALINDA   He *has* been rather – *unkind*!

ALFRED   Unkind! His behaviour has been monstrous.

Not *supper*?

ROSALINDA   (*Breaks* R) I thought perhaps a glass of wine . . .

ALFRED   (*Turning to her*) You think of *everything*. A dressing-gown – a smoking cap.
And to think how nervous I was of being alone with my goddess for the first time . . .! I never expected to be made at home like this!

ROSALINDA   (*Astonished*) Whatever are you doing?

ALFRED   What seems the most natural thing in the world. I'm taking over the duties of that profligate!

ROSALINDA   His d-d-duties . . .?

You will notice that the acting edition makes Alfred don the dressing-gown on his line 'I'm taking over the duties . . .' I found his next speech matched the business to the lines and substituted the move accordingly. He puts on the dressing-gown.

Alfred must not register Rosalinda's next line, and is engaged in tying the cord of the dressing-gown. Rosalinda is afraid that matters are going too far! She widens the gap between Alfred and herself by moving to the chair DR. *She can also use this for support.*

ALFRED   You'll be surprised how naturally I slip into them!

ROSALINDA   (*With raised eyebrows*)
Surprised is hardly the word!

ALFRED   (*Putting on smoking cap*)

Now how about a little supper darling
wife?

*This invariably gets a laugh and his line should
be held.*
*If necessary he can study the contents of the
table.*

ROSALINDA   (*Doubtfully*) Darling *wife*?

ALFRED   (*Inspecting the table; Foie gras* – a
cold capon – (*he picks at it*) – (*picking up
champagne bottle from the cooler*) and a
bottle of pink champagne. Delicious. I
have to be rather particular what I eat.

ROSALINDA   Oh, you *do*, do you?

ALFRED   My voice you know.
(*He sings a scale*)

Now, as for breakfast . . .

ROSALINDA   Breakfast?

*The acting edition makes Alfred sit here, but I
prefer to keep him standing for greater
mobility.*
Things are certainly getting out of hand!
*Here, as already noted, the food must be in
pre-planned positions. The capon is under a
dish cover, and has some edible portions laid by.*

ALFRED   Love gives one the appetite of a
god. All the same I must be careful.
Just some lightly boiled eggs – a dish
of sweetbreads – a little fish – a slice of
ham – a toasted roll or two . . .

Over his shoulder, inspecting the bottle.
*Rosalinda is now fuming and her manner
changes to an icy tone. It is amusing if Alfred
can run his 'Now as for breakfast' on from
the end of his vocalizing.*
*He must be prepared to complete this
sentence, Rosalinda really cuts in.*

Turning to her for once.

*He starts to unfasten the foil covering of the
champagne bottle.*

ROSALINDA   (*Cutting in*) Don't imagine
that you're going to breakfast *here*.

ALFRED   You would rather go out, my
love?

ROSALINDA   (x *to Alfred*) You'll be going
out – and long before breakfast, too!
(x *below sofa to* DR.) Do you want to
destroy my reputation entirely?

*It is a good plan to accelerate as Alfred runs
through the list.*

Very annoyed now, and she sweeps upstage R.
*Alfred, engrossed with the cork, tosses his
reply over his shoulder. Rosalinda makes a
strong, angry move to him.*

*Here again I have altered the moves as
suggested by the acting edition. Alfred has at
last been made aware of Rosalinda's disturbed
frame of mind.*
She stands DR *her back to him, her finger
drumming angrily on the back of the seat.*
*He has been halted in his business of opening
the bottle.*

ALFRED   (*Aside, front*) I can see that I
have been a little impetuous. I should
have let things take their course.
(*Aloud*) Do not worry, Rosalinda mine.

He opens the bottle with a 'pop'.

Returns bottle to the cooler.

He ends on a wide appeal.
Rosalinda turns sharply.

She turns away R.

(*He pours two glasses of champagne.*) The night is still young, let us live for the moment. Let us say that I am here just to take a glass of wine with you (*turns* DL) and *sing*?

ROSALINDA   No, no, not *that*!

ALFRED   (*Petulantly*) Not sing! But you used to like my voice?

ROSALINDA   Unfortunately I liked it too much, but tonight . . .

ALFRED   (X, *trying to embrace her*) My angel! Come to my arms. This is the moment of which your foolish, adoring Alfred has always dreamed!

ROSALINDA   (*Quick* X *to* DL. *Below Alfred.*) I think perhaps you had better *sing* after all!

I do not suggest that the interpretation given in this analysis is the definitive one; it is merely quoted as an example of the mechanics of blocking.

BLOCKING THE CHORUS MOVES

Let us now consider an example of ensemble blocking. I have selected a number from *White Horse Inn*, the London Amateur Premier of which I produced at the now defunct Finsbury Park Empire. (The musical number I intend to consider is No 4, 'Arrival of Guests', which will be found on pages 27 to 35 in the vocal score.)

The show is played mainly in a standing set, depicting the exterior of the White Horse Inn. The backcloth shows Lake Wolfgangsee and the mountains in the distance. The inn occupies stage left while on the opposite side stands the mayor's house.

During this vocal number, the guests arrive by the lake steamer and are greeted by the maids from the White Horse Inn, the porters from various local hotels, and Alpine guides and flower girls who are trying to sell their services and wares.

The first problem is the steamer! This is a built-up piece of scenic-ware mounted on a truck, which is propelled across the back of the set at the appropriate time. I was lucky in having friends in Austria who gave me details of the actual White Horse Inn and I was delighted to learn that the landing stage at the hotel was quite a distance away. I decided therefore that it was both permissible and logical to let the steamer dock off stage UR; its passage across the lake being indicated by the maids in the preceding dialogue. This gave me extra stage space, which even at the Empire was at a premium, and allowed the electric ground rows an un-obstructed throw onto the backcloth. The finalized ground plan for this show therefore became as in fig. 8.

Turning to the score, we find that this number requires a double chorus! We shall need maids (sopranos), Alpine guides (1st and 2nd tenors), flower girls (1st and 2nd contralto) and porters (baritone and basses) as well as another chorus, comprising all these voices, to play the various guests.

The best voices should be chosen for the maids, guides, flower girls and porters, since these sections sing separately. At the same time the heights of these parts must be considered. Ideally we shall require at least:

10 Maids who should be petite

6 Alpine guides who should look like outdoor types (and have good knees, as they wear *lederhosen*!)

6 Flower girls, who can be rather more buxom

7 Porters, who should be tall and commanding, plus Franz

The rest of the chorus, say eighteen, can be of assorted voices and shapes, while in addition we must keep in reserve a bride and bridegroom who make a brief entrance at the end of the number.

The same symbols that we used for the principals will again be used, and the various groups indicated as follows:

Maids   – A, B, C, D, E, F, G, H, I, J
Alpine guides – I, II, III, IV, V, VI
Flower girls   – a, b, c, d, e, f
Porters   – 1, 2, 3, 4, 5, 6, 7 plus Franz
Tourists   – T

Before the number starts, the maids have been told to clean up the inn, and they all have matching dusters. There are two bars introduction which illustrate, rather well, the shaking of a duster. The same rhythm occurs in bars 7 and 8. So we start the number with the maids flicking their dusters and moving to position

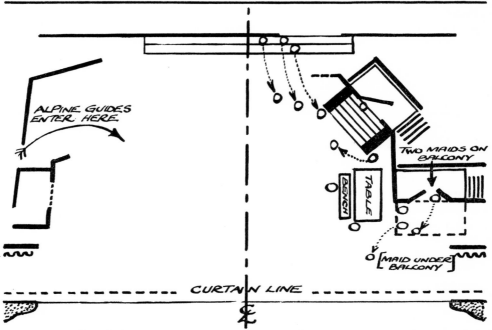

FIG 8   Details of chorus moves for a sequence from *White Horse Inn* (see also figs. 9-13).

as indicated in fig. 8. Whilst they sing they hold their dusters by the diagonal corners. On 'Heigh ho' they throw up their hands in mock despair, and at the end of their section (4 bars before fig. 2) go back to their dusting.

Now follow the Alpine guides, but if we let them enter as they sing, we shall lose a lot of the volume and also risk the chance of a bad vocal attack. We must put their entrance back a little, and the most suitable place is as the maids sing '. . . for the chambermaid'. Counting two steps per bar, this will get them eight steps on stage, in full view of the musical director before they have to sing. Their

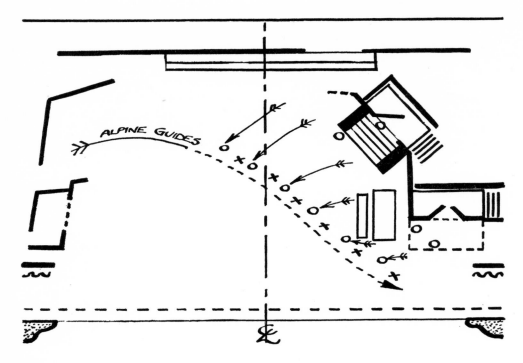

FIG 9

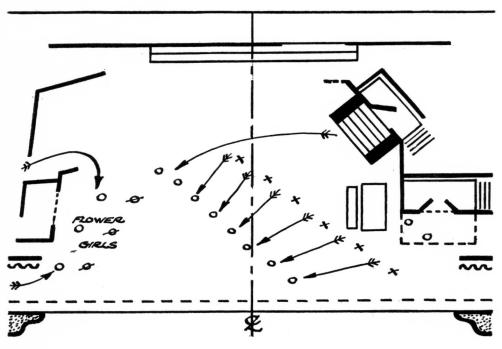

FIG 10

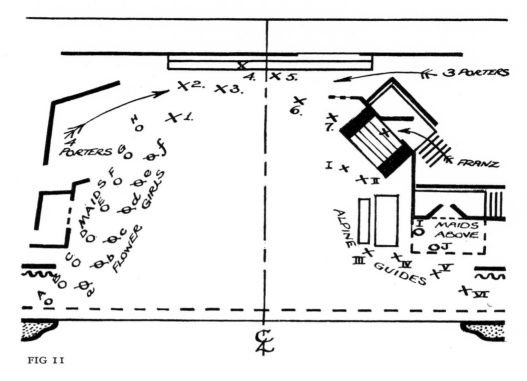

FIG 11

music has a strong march beat and their entrance should have a swagger. Their thumbs are thrust in their braces and they sing lustily, attracting the maids who break off their work and come down to them (fig. 9).

The flower girls have a gentler tune, and four bars of introduction. Their entrance can be far more leisurely. They carry baskets of flowers and they group DR. The maids leave the men and cross to admire the blooms (fig. 10).

Both the guides and the flower girls enter R which has been established as the direction of the village.

The porters have no introductory bars to their section and their entrance must be brought forward. They can enter severally and in a leisurely fashion, from both UR and UL (fig. 11).

At fig. 5 in the score, the counter melodies get complicated and it is advisable to keep the picture static and concentrate on the singing. After all, these characters have assembled to greet the guests, not to sell to each other! On the musical director's advice, I kept the voices in groups here.

At fig. 8 in the score, the guests arrive. This point is usually the cue for the rest of the chorus to burst onto the scene; but analyse this entrance. We have a collection of various ages, sexes and nationalities who have arrived at Wolfgang, for a holiday. Some have been here before, and know their way around, others are strangers, temporarily lost, some are having language difficulties, and most are carrying luggage. So the entrances will vary in speed and character and the music from fig. 8 to one bar before fig. 10 can be utilized for this movement. As the guests enter, the maids, porters, guides, and flower girls mill around, seeking their clients, whilst the music grows to a crescendo. A scene of energetic turmoil. Here are the suggested moves as listed in my score; each is cued to a specific bar of music.

1 Porter 1, meets two tourists, a man and a woman, and, with flower girls E, F, crosses DL to meet guide VI

Lady stays with porter and guide, man with flower girls

2 Maids a, b, c, x to DLC
3 Porter 2, meets two tourists, man and woman; joined by guide I and all x DR
  Man joins flower girls A, B
4 Two lady tourists enter x DLC. Meet maids a, b, c. Sit on cases
5 Porter 3 meets three lady tourists. Conducts them to LC where they are met
  by guide V
6 Porter 4 meets tourist lady, joined by guide II and they x RC
7 Two tourists x to Franz on steps of hotel
8 Porter 5 meets one tourist, conducts to ULC and met by guide IV
9 Flower girls CD meet two male tourists and take UC
10 Porter 6 and guide III meet female tourist and take URC

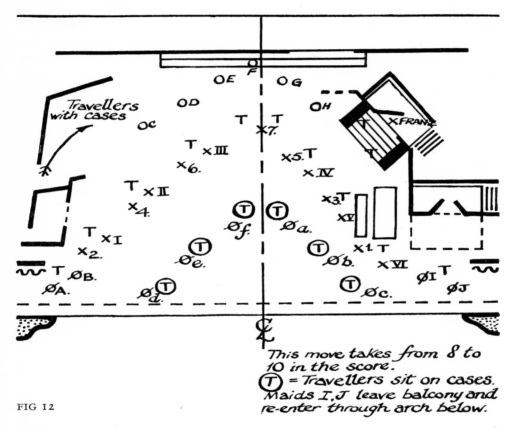

FIG 12

This move takes from 8 to
10 in the score.
Ⓣ = Travellers sit on cases.
Maids I, J leave balcony and
re-enter through arch below.

This looks very complicated, but rehearse it slowly and gradually, with repetition, and you will find the moves flow quite naturally. It is essential to work out mass movements in detail like this, so that every member of the ensemble knows exactly what he or she should do (fig. 12).

The picture should be held at fig. 10 in the score for the final repeat of the chorus, which is lusty. We could finish with this grouping, but a final move will underline the climax, so at the first bar on page 35, the seated characters rise on 'we raise our fees', pick up their cases on the 3rd bar 'and that's why you hear' and on bar 5 move to positions as fig. 13.

They halt in these positions on the last line, cases are placed on the floor and there is a general appeal.

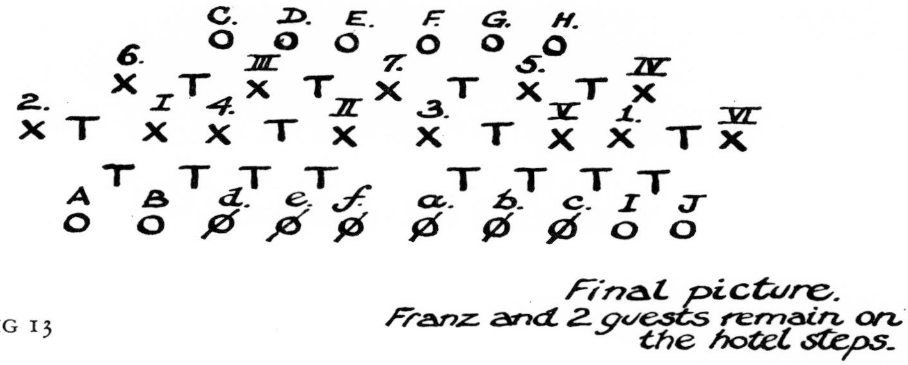

C. D. E. F. G. H.

6. 2. III 4. 7. II 5. 3. V 1. IV VI

A B d. e. f. a. b. c. I J

FIG 13

Final picture.
Franz and 2 guests remain on
the hotel steps.

One last point. The vocal line in the score ends on a short note, a quaver, and the orchestra continues with a strain from the 'Wedding March' to announce the arrival of the bride and groom. This music is usually drowned by the audience applause (or should be!) and the musical director and I therefore decided to make the last note, 'year', a minim and give a pause mark to the note to round off the vocal portion with a good climax. The orchestra cut off completely until brought in by the musical director; the 'Wedding March' was easily heard and the allusion to the bride and groom, who entered here, was clearly made.

DIALOGUE OVER MUSIC

Finally let us consider the question of dialogue over music. The forms can range from a simple *leitmotif* used to introduce a character, such as the melodramatic chords that announce the villain in a melodrama, to the complicated quasi-operatic finales such as the one that ends Act 1 of *Rose Marie*.

Before attempting to block any moves get to know the music; for indeed many of the themes will relate to the various characters or events. Sometimes the rhythm of the dialogue will be indicated in the music staves, but more often only the cue words will appear.

I recommend the following method when plotting dialogue over music. First, pencil the complete passage of dialogue into the score. Study it until you know the meaning of the lines. Then, listen to the music, try to pick out any relevant themes, any dramatic pauses, any changes of tempo – see what the music has to say. Finally, put words and music together.

Let us consider as an example part of the finale of Act 1 of *Rose Marie*. The relevant pages are 87 to 89 in the vocal score as published by Chappell and Company Limited.

After the trio which starts the finale, we hear the Mountie's theme (*poco marcato*). Malone and the Mounties approach, as indicated in the score, and Rose Marie has a visual cue for her cry 'Malone!'

At *moderato* on page 88 is the 'My Jim' theme and this I suggest is the cue for the dialogue which Rose Marie introduces with 'You've always been my friend'. I have put this line forward by one bar, to coincide with the theme. There are ample pauses and breaks in this passage to cover all the dialogue until Emile speaks. His line is given as indicated in the score, but, unless he intends to drag out this short speech (which is surely against his character) I have found the bars marked *molto sostenuto* fit better if played *moderato*, ignoring all the pauses, the chord in the ¼ bar coming before Rose Marie's 'What's that you say?'

At *con molto sentimento* the 'Jim' theme appears again and this covers the dialogue to Lady Jane's entrance.

The Indian theme, *molto moderato quasi lento* refers to the speeches concerning the death of Black Eagle and the *ad libitum* bar continues until Malone's 'Wanda saw him do it'.

Andante molto is the Mounties' theme again and covers Malone's instructions to his men.

Rose Marie tries once more to save her lover – 'Malone, no use to look etc' at the top of page 89, *plaintively*, and this runs easily into Emile's line at *moderato*. Some careful timing is necessary after this in order that Rose Marie's cry from the heart, 'Please', coincides with the pause chord in the *presto* bar. From here to the vocal line on page 90 must be very carefully timed so that Rose Marie can speak into her singing. The music must flow quietly under the dialogue, and there are only four pauses indicated to assist the musical director. There should be only the briefest of gaps between Rose Marie's 'Care for him' and her 'Like ev'ry girl in all de worl' '.

Once the actors have established the speed of their dialogue in a passage such as this, they should be instructed to maintain it at all performances in order that the musical director may know what to expect and control his orchestra accordingly. As rehearsals progress you will find that the actors will know instinctively whether they are in time or not and they will adjust accordingly.

3 Casting the show

'. . . show me!'
MY FAIR LADY

INTRODUCTION

A good cast of principals is an essential ingredient to the success of any production. Choosing one is a phase of production most subject to chance and one that taxes the judgement and experience of the production team to the full. From their initial conferences the producer, musical director and choreographer will have decided upon the probable physical appearance of the characters and the alternative ways in which they may be portrayed.

Do not be too dogmatic in your conception of the roles, since the choice of candidates is likely to be limited. Exceptions occur when the part to be played is a representation of an actual person. Emperor Franz Josef in *The White Horse Inn*, Cardinal Richelieu in *The Three Musketeers* and Franz Schubert in *Lilac Time* should be played by actors who must physically resemble these persons. However, I see no reason why Mr Snow in *Carousel* has to be played by a big man, simply because that was the way the part was cast in the Drury Lane production.

THE PROFESSIONAL'S APPROACH

Here let us consider the approach of the professional producer to the task of casting a show. Having decided exactly how he wants the parts portrayed, he can go out and look for the player who fits all his requirements. He is limited only by the extent of his budget and the time at his disposal. Indeed many a professional production is set aside until the chosen artist is free to undertake the engagement.

The professional producer can call on the services of casting agencies, his own knowledge of possible candidates' performances in other productions and the *Actor's Year Book* as well as hold as many auditions as he thinks fit. From all these sources he prepares a short list of likely applicants and it is from this list that the final line-up is usually selected.

The amateur producer is invariably short of time, candidates and money to indulge his ideas on presentation and auditions are often a matter of compromise. He has to learn to 'cut his coat according to his cloth', since societies will often insist on presenting shows which are way above their talents and technical ability to produce, but it is this challenge of attempting the near impossible that spurs the amateur producer on to greater achievements.

AUDITIONS – PROCEDURE

Auditions should be held as soon as possible after the selection of a new show to allow the musical director ample time to rehearse the principals' music and integrate them with the chorus in the ensembles. Auditions should be held in the actual theatre where the performances are to be played, or failing this, a hall of comparable size should be engaged for the occasion. An audience may be invited to help to create an atmosphere but opinions vary as to the advisability of this and it is a matter best decided by the general management committee in consultation with the production team.

The procedure adopted for auditions varies from one company to another, and the producer is advised to acquaint himself, in advance, with local custom, and arrange to alter any matter of which he may strongly disapprove.

A method used by many societies involves an audition committee, made up as follows:

Chairman, producer, musical director, choreographer
Two persons, not connected with the society, but who have a working knowledge of the show under discussion
Two members of the society, elected by the company
A member of the general management committee
The secretary of the society, *ex officio*, who takes notes and reports back to the general management committee.

This august body sit apart and at some distance from the stage – the front row of the dress circle is a good spot – the better to judge the ability of the various applicants. In addition, a pianist and two readers-in attend, the latter being invited from a local dramatic society to read the other parts in the short audition scenes.

Two or three weeks before auditions are to be held, the producer and musical director announce the selected passages of dialogue and vocal numbers to be heard. All members of the company should be encouraged to attempt a role. It can be pointed out to them that the audition committee are looking more for intelligent interpretation, lively imagination and the ability to think out and develop a part, than for a technically polished performance. Remember that many a light burns under a bushel in amateur groups, and that the greater the selection, the easier the task of the audition committee.

While the auditionee may need to refer to the score for vocal auditions, he should be encouraged to memorize the passages of libretto and to invent moves and business, making full use of all his skills.

Should the part call for dancing, the choreographer may have to set a simple dance routine as a test piece. This can be kept short and merely serves as an indication of the applicant's dancing ability.

Parts are heard in order of importance; first the romantic leads, then the comedy part, the heavy character roles and so on. Every effort should be made to put auditionees at their ease: even the most hardened, experienced player suffers from nerves on these occasions. Sometimes it is a good plan to ignore the first few minutes of an audition and allow the applicant time to warm-up and overcome his initial nervousness and questions may be put by the committee on any point that may need clarification.

AUDITIONS — DISCUSSIONS

The discussions that follow the auditions give everyone a chance to air his views. Naturally those of the producer and his colleagues are the most important, but the production team should take note of the impressions and opinions of the rest of the committee. In the majority of cases, the choice of the candidate will be unanimous but when opinions are sharply divided, the final selection must rest with the producer, musical director and choreographer for it is they who ultimately produce the show.

In the main, the committee will arrive at its decisions on the basis of what they have seen, but there will be occasions when discussion reaches a deadlock. At this juncture it is, I believe, legitimate to introduce any other knowledge one may have of a candidate's ability. For example, it is well known that there are some actors who can give a first-class audition but who never improve on their initial reading; there are others who undergo agonies of nervous agitation at auditions, but who, in rehearsal, develop a character beyond one's highest hopes. One can also cite the artist who, while nominally a member of the company, will only play in a principal role, and if unsuccessful will look elsewhere for a part. This knowledge can often be used to resolve an *impasse* when opinions are equally divided between two contenders for a part.

Often one has to sacrifice the acting for the vocal ability or *vice versa*. Many a good comedy role has been played by an actor with little or no singing voice, and the musical director can compromise by letting the songs be taken *parlando*. I have no regrets at casting a first-class (non-singing) actor as Papa Veit in *Lilac Time*. His half-spoken delivery of the 'Girls and Boys' duet in Act 2 was exactly right and most moving, whereas a full-blooded baritone would have been completely out of character. Conversely, a really good top tenor is essential for the role of Sid-el-Kar in *Desert Song* and if the singer is an indifferent actor who cannot respond to intensive coaching, his part must be kept as simple as possible or even, in extreme circumstances, his lines divided among the other parts.

OTHER CONSIDERATIONS

Occasionally it may not be possible to cast a part at all, either because there are no applicants or because auditionees do not come up to the required standard. In such cases one must look elsewhere for a suitable actor and I strongly urge the producer to oppose any pressure from the general management committee to make him select from their society. A producer must remember that his reputation is affected by every production that he undertakes and it is in his own interest and that of the society for which he produces, to keep his standards as high as he reasonably can. By maintaining a high standard, even at the expense of occasionally inviting outsiders to play, the company will attract fresh talent and enjoy a wider and better choice of potential principals from among their own numbers.

If one has to go outside the company to find a suitable actor, the knowledge of other companies' work is of great assistance. While watching other amateur productions the amateur producer should note the name of any artist whose performance impresses him. He should also endeavour to be on the closest terms with neighbouring societies since he will undoubtedly need their assistance at some time or another. The National Operatic and Dramatic Society is another source of assistance. Outsiders usually play by invitation but they are generally asked to give an audition, as a mere formality, in order to satisfy that they are of the required standard.

There is some dissension as to whether any direction should be given at auditions. Some instruction can often determine whether the applicant is able to pick up direction quickly and intelligently. It can also assist the musical director if he can test the full vocal range of a singer, or his ability to sing in concerted items with other principals.

Ideally, all principal roles should be understudied, but this is rarely possible for neither the producer nor the stage manager have the necessary time to rehearse them. Once again, with the assistance of Noda, a nearby company who have recently presented the show, may be asked to stand by during the week of the production, in case of mishap. The producer and choreographer will often be sufficiently talented to be able to step into a part if the actor or actress falls ill, but in any case all parts should be adequately covered.

4 Rehearsals · the first phase

'A thing I never lack is tact!'
GIPSY BARON

INTRODUCTION

We turn now to the producer's most important *raison d'être*, namely rehearsals and their conduct. Rehearsals fall into four groups:
  1 Music rehearsals, under the musical director
  2 Principal rehearsals
  3 Ensemble rehearsals
  4 Dancing rehearsals, under the choreographer
Before discussing these in detail we should consider the schedule of rehearsals. How long does the amateur company need to rehearse? As a guide, let us consider the number of hours that are necessary to mount a professional musical production, or rather a reproduction for a tour, since this represents a fairer comparison with the amateur company.

Intense and continuous rehearsals usually occupy a minimum of three weeks prior to dress rehearsals. An eight-hour day is often augmented with evening music rehearsals or coaching sessions and the total number of rehearsal hours works out like this:

Principals	119 hours
Chorus	77 hours
Dancers	77 hours

Compare these times with those of an average amateur operatic society that presents two productions a year:

Principals	65 hours
Chorus	93 hours
Dancers	54 hours

They indicate that the amateur rarely gets what a trained professional would regard as the minimum rehearsal time. Moreover, the amateur does not usually indulge in *continuous* rehearsal, his sessions often being two or three days apart. All the more reason then for the producer to plan in advance and to utilize every minute of rehearsal time to the best effect.

THE PRODUCER AS A TEACHER

There are three reasons for rehearsals; experiment, teaching and polishing. Amateurs, with their business commitments and other interests, rarely have the time for much experiment; they rely on the producer to experiment and plot the show for them before rehearsals actually start. The producer of amateur musicals will discover that most of his rehearsal time will be taken up with the second stage and that he acts in the capacity of a teacher rather than a producer.

It is strange how few members of the average operatic group consider that any training is necessary. They will willingly put in long hours of private practice to improve their golf handicap, or perfect their forehand drive or their bowling prowess, but, apart from the regular rehearsal nights, they rarely undertake any private practice to perfect their singing, speech, deportment, or any of the many facets that go to make a competent all-round player.

However, the producer must assume that his actors want to be taught and help them in every possible way. He should aim at inducing in his cast – principals and chorus alike – a desire to learn and assimilate the substance and the principles of acting and singing, and not merely the technique.

Think big The producer should teach his actors to think in terms of shows, not parts; in scenes, not lines, and in the composite stage picture, not individual movements and business. He must also stress the importance of *playing big* when acting in musicals. The techniques used in straight plays can still be used, but they must be broader.

Analyse The producer should teach his cast how to analyse a play; to search for the reasons for the behaviour of a character, and his relationship to other characters in the show; to assess the mood and rhythm of each scene, and to appreciate the style of the piece.

Basic principles The producer should teach the basic principles of movement and business. The most important of these are listed below:

1 An actor should always face the audience when speaking. This need not be taken too literally, but it is well to remember that once the direction of the actor's delivery comes upstage of the proscenium opening, as much as sixty per cent of his projection and volume will be lost to the audience

2 All important scenes should be played downstage. The most important place on the stage is DC and one's importance diminishes as one gets farther from this position

3 Movements should follow straight lines

4 An actor entering should come well on-stage and not linger in the entrance

5 When two characters, in conversation, make an entrance, the speaker should enter last and downstage of the other

6 Exits should be made on a line

7 Movements should start on the upstage foot

8 Turns should usually be made downstage, towards the audience

9 When an actor is required to kneel on one knee, it should be his downstage knee

10 When a man and woman embrace, the man's downstage arm should be below the woman's and his upstage arm above hers. This allows the woman's face to be towards the audience

There are other rules and, naturally, all of them are made to be broken, but they are distilled from a great deal of wisdom and experience. The actor who learns the reasons for these traditional rules will also learn to recognize when they may be safely broken!

Keeping in character   The producer should teach his actors how to remain in character, even when they are not speaking. He must teach the art of repose as well as how to respond to other characters without distracting from them. He must help them to sense the balance of the scene, both visually and orally and to know when to dominate and when to yield the stage.

'For the first time'   The producer should teach his actors to cultivate what William Gillette has termed 'the illusion of the first time': to give the impression that what they are saying is spontaneous and not a series of memorized lines. Apart from all this, the producer should also encourage his actors to seek further instruction in fields that he cannot cover: singing lessons, dancing classes, fencing classes and voice-production lessons. He should encourage them to read on all aspects of dramatic art, to listen intelligently to recordings of great singers, to appreciate good professional productions of both musicals and straight plays. This is a huge task, limited only by the time available, the degree of enthusiasm of the actors and the ability of the producer to stimulate the interest.

Now to consider the different rehearsals in detail.

MUSIC REHEARSALS

For many years it has been my good fortune to be associated with Sydney Lockerman. Before taking up the baton as musical director for the Wood Green Operatic Society Sydney was an actor and chorus master and I am indebted to him for the following remarks relating to the musical side of operatic productions.

It must be realized that a musical director of an amateur operatic society is on duty from the first note of a music rehearsal until the final chord of the last performance. Some societies have a chorus master to teach the notes with the musical director attending final rehearsals to polish and blend the whole show. The former arrangement is to be preferred as it enables the musical director to 'live' with the show from start to finish. If this method is adopted the following procedures are suggested:

1 Assume that no member of the society can read music and teach each note of every part so that it is committed to memory

2 Do not work too fast and make sure that all members know their notes

3 If entrance auditions are held (which is advisable) be very careful to place the entrant in the correct voice range: 1st soprano, 2nd soprano, 1st alto, 2nd alto, 1st tenor, 2nd tenor, baritone or bass

(This is important as some scores call for these sub-divisions and it must be assumed that once an entrant has been accepted he or she will stay with the society for many shows)

4 One has to work to a dead-line – that being when the producer starts staging. It is better, therefore, to complete the score as quickly as possible, learning the correct notes and adding dynamics once this has been done. It is usually

found that once the notes and words have been mastered and memorized the musical director can adjust the interpretation at a later date. If one is conducting such works as *Die Fledermaus* or *The Gipsy Baron* one cannot play them in strict tempo. The dynamics in these works are absolutely essential. Accents and phrasing must be observed

5 It is most important to have a good accompanist since he can ease the lot of a musical director considerably

Once the cast has been selected it is useful to hold music rehearsals for the principals and these can be in private houses. It is important for the musical director to run through the whole of the principals' work so they have a clear picture of what is required. Phrasing should be marked in the score at the first rehearsal so that the number can be practised according to the musical director's markings.

When the principals know their numbers, they should be sung at full rehearsals. This method allows the chorus to hear music in which they are not involved and at the same time it tries out the principals in front of an audience.

Thus with chorus and principals rehearsing separately and then being brought together the entire score has been covered. It is up to the musical director during rehearsals to decide when the company should start memorizing the score. Obviously, the sooner the better as it is his responsibility to ensure that when staging begins, the score is known by heart.

The musical director should be prepared for the fact that some of the music may be forgotten while the company is learning stage movement; it is therefore useful to have one or two music-only rehearsals during the later period of staging.

It is of the utmost importance for the producer, musical director and choreographer to work as a team and in complete harmony.

During rehearsals questions will inevitably arise concerning such details as tempo, interpretation and staging. These should be fully discussed by the production team as they occur and any changes implemented only after such discussion and when they serve to improve the show as a whole.

PRINCIPALS' REHEARSAL

The first reading Once the principal parts are selected, it is a good plan to have a reading of the play with them. Some producers – W. S. Gilbert was one – like to read the play to the cast themselves; others allow the actors to read their own parts. The latter course is not always successful, for actors are not necessarily good readers. However, it is the method I use and I generally take the cast through the entire work, omitting all musical items, but giving all the cuts and alterations.

Since a good half of the show is musical, the reading does not take long, and time can be devoted to discussion of the play – the style in which it is to be played, the characters and the settings, so that, from the very start, the principals have the finished production in mind.

Once the principals have read through with the producer, they can, if time allows, repeat the process before the whole company. Musical illustrations can be added, with comments by the producer and the musical director, so that the company can visualize the overall production and see the parts in context.

Blocking out The next step is the 'blocking out' process. If the producer has prepared his prompt-book along the lines already discussed he will find his task considerably eased. The purpose of blocking-out rehearsals is to give the actors something clear and correct to study. The producer must impress upon his actors the necessity for private practice, and blocking out merely sets the foundation for this homework.

The rehearsal starts with a detailed description of the setting. This can be done with model sets or black-board diagrams, both of which are useful adjuncts to what is in my opinion the best method, namely to lay out the set, full size, on the rehearsal floor. Tape, chalk or chairs can be used to indicate the boundaries of the setting as well as the entrances and exits. The actual furniture which will be used, or objects as near to their exact size should be used.

The producer proceeds to take his actors through a French scene, letting them walk their parts and encouraging them to make copious notes in their libretto of all moves and business.

It is generally assumed that principals understand the nomenclature of the various parts of the stage (see fig. 14), and stage directions, that they underline their lines as a matter of course, and have evolved their own form of shorthand to assist note taking. However, it is worthwhile checking on these points at the first rehearsal, since there are invariably newcomers to parts and a few introductory words to these beginners will be of value.

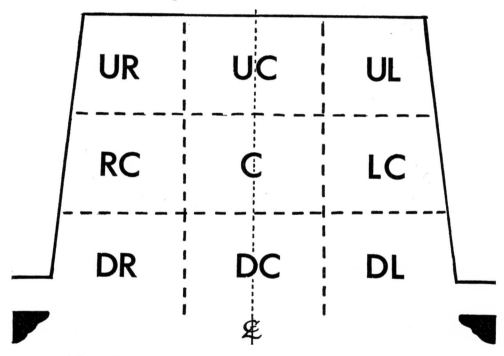

FIG 14   The main acting areas

No hand properties are used at these early rehearsals, nor is continuity of any importance. Indeed, since musical shows generally involve a long list of speaking parts it is often necessary to take sections of unrelated libretto in order to give everyone something to do. The important thing is to give each some work, see that your directions are clearly understood, and send them away to learn it!

Memorizing the words   This raises the question of how soon the words should be committed to memory. A professional actor is often required to learn a part in a week. The manner in which he achieves this is a purely mechanical process, and the professional usually has enough technical knowledge of his art to be able to differentiate between the *words* and the *meaning*. On the other hand, if the amateur starts learning his part before the producer has had a chance to discuss and block the scenes he may well come up with business and an interpretation contrary to that desired by the producer and he will often find great difficulty in unlearning his mistakes. For this reason, I insist that my cast do not commit lines to memory until I have blocked out a scene and am satisfied that they understand the meaning and the moves. Once this point is established – and it should be as quickly as possible – the actor can undertake the memorizing of lines. There are various aids to help get rid of the book. The very act of reading lines whilst walking through the moves and business is one; others include writing out the pages of dialogue concerned (all the speeches, not only the actor's part) using a tape-recorder or reading the script prior to sleep. The individual must find the way that suits him best, for until the books are laid aside, the next stage of rehearsing cannot begin. I recommend that the producer announce, well in advance, the deadline, after which no scripts will be permitted at rehearsals.

Experiment   This period of rehearsal is one of experiment – the producer is confirming that his initial plotting and interpretation is both logical and practical; the actors are groping their way to a basic understanding of their parts. Consequently, discussion should be encouraged, though, where possible, this is better left to the end of the evening over a coffee or a drink. Indeed I have found these after-rehearsal sessions extremely useful and many valid suggestions and arguments have been propounded in a spirit of co-operative enthusiasm.

If the producer should find it necessary to alter or amend any of his initial planning (and which producer does not?) the corrections should be entered in his prompt-book for future reference.

As rehearsals proceed it will be possible to allocate time for revision. A good plan is to utilize the first part of the evening to blocking new scenes, in preparation for the week's homework, and to spend the last hour in polishing work already learned. Once the entire libretto has been blocked and committed to memory, the vocal numbers can be staged. These will have already been rehearsed by the musical director for their musical interpretation and technique, and now the producer has to incorporate them in the show and block them in the same way as he did the libretto. Certain points must be borne in mind when setting moves for a vocal number. Where possible, the singer should remain static, gestures, which should be broad, should be used only where they are essential and to give added point to a phrase. When moves and business are required they should not constrict the singer's diaphragm or turn him upstage so that his voice fails to project. Every effort should be made to allow the singer to be as far downstage as possible; bear in mind that once a singer or actor turns upstage of the proscenium arch, up to sixty per cent of his projection is lost to the audience. Any principals who have to dance will be taken by the choreographer to learn their routines, and by the time of the first scheduled run-through, the principals should have a good basic knowledge both of their parts and of the show.

The chorus   While the principals have been rehearsing, the chorus have been learning the score with the musical director, and the time has now come to turn our attention to their staging. By the time the producer requires them they should have memorized the music and words of all the ensembles. This is vital, since most of chorus business is cued to a certain musical phrase or word and if the chorus member is struggling to recall the score, he will certainly not be able to take the producer's direction. As Sydney Lockerman pointed out, the quality and interpretation of the musical items will suffer at the early staging rehearsals, but, provided the ground work has been firmly established, a 'polishing' rehearsal will soon remedy these short-comings.

Nearly every book dealing with production urges the producer to be patient, and even-tempered, especially when dealing with amateurs. Ideally, this should be so; but I must confess that, when dealing with the ensemble, it is often a very difficult dictum to follow. In the hope that some chorus members read this book, I list a few sure ways to break a producer's heart!

1 Be unpunctual for rehearsals. This will usually necessitate the producer repeating his directions for a difficult ensemble and endear you to your fellow choristers

2 Be an irregular attender at rehearsals, either cutting them without notice or giving trifling excuses – 'I'm going to the cinema'. This is what Dolman says of such people: 'People who prefer some other form of pleasure to acting, or even to rehearsing, have a perfect right to their preference, but they have no place in the theatre'

3 Be inattentive at rehearsals, either indulging in loud conversation, knitting or even 'popping across to the local'. Such people not only distract the members actually working but they do not assimilate their own parts

4 Act the comic, seizing every opportunity to crack a joke and indulge in horseplay

5 Appoint yourself a co-producer and so prove your interest. You can be constantly correcting your fellow artists and pointing out to the producer a better way of doing things. Luckily for producers, these types do not usually last long!

There are other ways to wreak havoc, and let no one suppose that such irresponsible attitudes are found only in the ranks of the amateur theatre. The difference is that the professional producer can voice his disapproval in no uncertain terms whilst the producer of amateurs is expected to restrain his feelings. I recommend my fellow producers to make matters quite clear at the initial rehearsal, explaining that the show is a team effort and depends for its success on the co-operation of *every single member*. Remember, there are no small parts, only small actors!

This will mean that the producer will have to ensure that he himself attends rehearsals punctually, with his plan of rehearsals clearly worked out in advance – another reason for careful preparation of the prompt-book! Start on time – even if there are only half a dozen members present; I assure you that once the company realize you are a man of your word, they will become punctual and regular attenders.

A problem with chorus members is the retention of their moves and business from one rehearsal to the next. They should be encouraged to write their directions over the appropriate bars in their scores, and instructed to look over the work before attending the next rehearsal.

Often the entire ensemble is not required for a number, and it is possible to arrange for the ladies only to attend at the usual rehearsal time, the men coming an hour later. Taking this arrangement turn and turn about does allow the busy housewife or businessman to get to rehearsals in a leisurely fashion and will be appreciated by them.

The co-operation of the management committee of the society should be sought, to keep down the available noise at rehearsals, to keep tea breaks and notices to a minimum so that all time is used to the best advantage.

Principals, when not required for an ensemble, should be encouraged to utilize the time in private practice in an adjoining room.

Producing the chorus   Chorus work falls broadly into two main types. There is the regimented, routine number, usually found in the older musical comedy. The soldiers chorus in *Desert Song*, and the 'Entrance of the Peers' in *Iolanthe* are cases in point. The other style is what I term individual cameo work and occurs when the chorus is made up of a lot of individual characters – the sailors in 'Bloody Mary,' *South Pacific*, the rabble in *Vagabond King* and the chorus throughout *Oklahoma* and *Carousel* are examples. Often both styles will appear in the same show and the technique for directing these scenes should be varied accordingly.

When staging an ensemble number first consider whether it is merely an interpolated chorus or an essential part of the story, carrying on and expanding the plot. Having decided the purpose of the number, consider whether to keep the various voice groups together, especially if the chorus is a difficult one with complex inter-scoring. Grouping the vocal parts together will give the musical director firm control over the various sections and make for easy cueing, but it can inhibit the moves and groupings that the producer may wish to set. However, when dealing with a young, inexperienced cast I recommend this method.

Now consider the heights of the cast. Generally place the tallest upstage and at the sides, with the shorter ones dressing the more central areas. This avoids masking and allows the cast to see the musical director. A method I frequently employ for grouping the chorus is what I term the pyramid method. Allowing an infinite number of variations, it is, as the name implies, based on triangles. To give a simple illustration: place three people in a triangle, a tall man in the centre with two shorter women either side and slightly downstage of him. Whether viewed from stalls or circle this presents a triangle to the audience. Any number of people can be used in this method and the triangles can be of varied shapes and sizes and be incorporated into larger ones. The individual triangles/pyramids should have a relationship to each other so that the entire stage becomes one vast pyramidic composition. Always plan in the round, viewing your groups from all angles and from above, making sure that a satisfying and aesthetic picture is achieved from all parts of the theatre.

The movements and business in the regimented routine are planned like a military drill sequence. Actions are timed to occur on certain cue words, and the routine is practised again and again until this military precision is achieved. Cues should always be given on the strong beat in the bar, and gestures should be big, made from the shoulder using the whole arm. Amateurs tend to make small, mean gestures from the elbow, which look ugly. Attention should be paid to the follow-through. Teach the chorus to use all the music so that one movement flows naturally into the next and does not appear to be a series of unrelated jerks. Keep the eyes and heads up and encourage singing to the back of the theatre.

The modern musical calls for a looser treatment of the chorus. In these, each individual must be a character, reacting and playing within that character whilst being part of the ensemble. After explaining to the company the context and purpose of the scene and describing the action, the chorus is placed in position. Now some individual instruction is necessary; explain clearly to each group what types of characters they are, how they are involved in the action, and what their probable reactions will be. Cue words are allocated for entrances and important moves, but the individual groups are encouraged to think out the detail of their actions. I find it better to get the company to overplay at first – it is easy to get them to play down once the sequence is established, but it can be very difficult to broaden the parts. Moreover, it gives the producer an idea of an individual's capabilities – whether they can imagine their characters from the brief sketch he has given them or whether they will require detailed private tuition. Since time is always at a premium, the more that the individual can give, the easier the producer's task and the better the spontaneity of the show.

Rabbles, market scenes, the natural-seeming coming and goings in a busy street scene have to be meticulously thought-out; entrances and exits timed to definite cues; actual paths of movement defined – properties and stage business checked for authenticity. We should seek for a rhythm to the ebb and flow of the whole action, but should the eye linger on one spot, there should still be discernible the individual characters who, together, make up a homogeneous whole.

Chorus members can be highly inhibited when it comes to mime, and it is often necessary to break down their reserve. A warming-up or limbering-up process before actually beginning to stage a sequence is useful, especially if the business can be carried out in a spirit of fun. A simple example that I have used to break down this wall of shyness and reserve is to have the chorus form two lines, facing each other. I tell them to take a deep breath and as they exhale, to say 'Ha, ha, ha' fairly quickly. In no time at all they are laughing at each other; inhibitions vanish and what is more, they have learned the basic method of laughing to order. Encourage the members to observe and to draw upon their own experiences for their mimes.

DANCING REHEARSALS

Many producers are also accomplished choreographers and undertake the setting and rehearsal of all the dance routines in addition to their other duties. Such producers are an asset to a company, particularly in such modern shows as *West Side Story*. However, whilst a practical knowledge of stage dancing is an advantage, it is by no means an essential part of a producer's make-up. What he will need is a sympathetic understanding of the choreographer's task, and the ability to express his ideas for the choreographer to produce in terms of the dance.

A good choreographer or dancing mistress is a tower of strength to the producer. Working in close collaboration with him, she can not only devise, rehearse and perfect the dance routines, but she can also polish ensembles that the producer has already blocked, and often take over an entire rehearsal in the event of the producer's illness.

Few operatic societies are fortunate enough to have an established dance troupe, nor can they always call upon the services of a local ballet school. Under an experienced resident dancing mistress, it is possible to build up a small nucleus of dancers over the years, but generally one has to search around for sufficient talent to make up the team. Certainly male dancers are a perennial problem, and the good male dancers who do not turn professional are usually in great demand and share their services among several local societies.

Nellie Lindsey, a professional dancing teacher and choreographer of amateur companies for many years puts her point of view:

'A dancing mistress must be, above all, an optimist! There are lots of average singers, but there is no such thing as an average dancer! They all fall into two categories – those that can dance and those that cannot!'

According to Nellie Lindsey, these are three main difficulties to overcome:

Getting sufficient dancers of the required standard The answer to this is to take the best of the talent available. Of these you will almost certainly find three or four good, trained dancers and it is around these that the dance routines will be planned. The non-dancers should be given very simple steps and movements and used to dress and decorate the stage. If necessary, cut the total number of dancers used in certain routines – better a team of six good, slick dancers than a dozen or more who are only second best.

Adequate stage space   This is a matter for discussion between producer and dancing mistress. Dancers need space, and it is often necessary to alter the positions of furniture to accommodate the dance. This should be borne in mind by the producer when preparing his prompt-book to allow for this to be done unobtrusively as part of the business of the scene. Sometimes, too, it may be advisable to allow some of the chorus to quit the scene, leaving a token number to dress the set, whilst a dance proceeds. These matters should be noted and discussed at the early planning conferences.

Details of dancer's costumes   When so many shows are booked with a costumier as a set, details of individual costumes – skirt lengths, colour combinations, head-dresses and so on, are rarely given unless specifically asked for. Where practical, the dancing mistress should make a point of seeing the actual costumes proposed for her dancers, so that she can set the style of her dance accordingly, or demand alternative dresses.

A dancing mistress will need a good accompanist at all her rehearsals, who should be fully conversant with the *tempi* which the musical director and choreographer have agreed on. It assists the choreographer if, when plotting the dances prior to rehearsals, she has a tape-recording of the dances, played at the proper *tempi* and with all cuts and alterations as agreed with the musical director.

Technical terms should generally be avoided with people trying to dance for the first time. '. . . this is just a waste of time. Speak to them in words that they can understand: to jump, to bend, to turn and so on, and use practical demonstration as much as possible.' (Nellie Lindsey)

Early dancing rehearsals can often be used to teach various steps in a style suitable for the show, later working them into a routine. This is one way to sort out the sheep from the goats, and gives the trained dancers a basis to work from, and a feeling of the particular style required for the show.

Nor need a routine be rehearsed in sequence. 'Often it is better to work small sections at a time and build the routine rather like a jigsaw puzzle. This makes the complete build up more interesting for those concerned and often gives the choreographer a chance to utilize her good dancers to better advantage.'

Above all, rehearse to perfection. A slick, well-rehearsed routine, however simple, will be appreciated by the majority of your audience, few of whom will know much about actual dancing technique.

5 Rehearsals · the second phase

'. . . Getting to know all about you.'
THE KING AND I

INTRODUCTION

Ordinarily the blocking out of a musical production, involving as it does the principals, chorus and dancers, may take as many as sixteen rehearsal sessions. During this period the producer will, naturally, be anxious to set as much of the show as possible, but he should allow some portion of each rehearsal for recapping on what has already been taught. He should also beware of devoting too much time to the first act at the expense of the rest of the show – a common fault in amateur production. I have, for many years, worked on the theory that, if the beginning and ending of each act of a musical are well rehearsed, the audience will more easily forgive a slight looseness of production in the middle of the act. I hasten to add that I endeavour to keep as high a standard as possible overall, but it is certainly true that if you can capture the interest of your audience at the rise of the curtain and end each act on a peak of enthusiasm you are more than half way home!

THE FIRST RUN-THROUGH

As soon as the whole show has been blocked, the producer should call his first run-through. Most companies find it convenient to hold this during the weekend, since a minimum of four hours is necessary in order to accomplish everything.

The full cast, including dancers and extras, or walk-ons, should be called, as well as the stage manager, the assistant stage manager, the effects man, property man, call-boy and prompter. The musical director and choreographer will, naturally, be in attendance.

Ideally, this rehearsal should be held in the theatre or hall where the actual performances will be given, but it is the lucky society who can get these premises, and usually a large rehearsal room has to suffice. An area should be marked out to correspond as nearly as possible to the actual settings that will be used – chairs, chalk or tape will serve to mark the limits of the stage. Furniture and properties should be used even though it is unlikely that the actual pieces that will be used in the performances will be available at this juncture.

The producer should watch the rehearsal from a seat in the centre of the stalls if possible. He should allow the cast to go right through the show without interruption, make copious notes (a capable short-hand writer to assist is a great boon) and save his remarks until the end.

The value of this reviewing rehearsal cannot be overstressed. It allows the whole production team a chance to appraise the overall state of the show and plan the next phase of rehearsals.

For the producer it should primarily reassure him that his cast has understood his directions and *nothing wrong is being learned*. It also allows him to see how his principals develop their parts as the show proceeds and whether they are beginning to work together as a team. He will be able to reappraise his chorus groupings and stage pictures bearing in mind the limitations of space, settings and lighting. Finally he can see whether the cast as a whole are interpreting the musical with the correct emphasis.

The musical director will be able to judge the timing of his cues for musical items, to note where principals or chorus need cues on a particularly tricky entry, and to assess how much the musical interpretation has degenerated during the initial staging rehearsals.

The choreographer will probably be seeing her dances integrated into the production for the first time. Her problems will revolve around questions of stage space, tempo, entrances, exits and stage pictures.

The stage manager and his assistants are also seeing the show as a whole for the first time. This will give them an opportunity to revise their plots, and cue sheets, check the positions of furniture and properties, get a rough timing on lighting, scene changes and on the initial running times of the various scenes.

The cast too, stand to gain a lot from this rehearsal. The various rehearsals of the past few weeks fall into place and they can see the show as a whole. If it is a production involving many costume changes, they will get an idea of the time available for them to effect these.

When the rehearsal is over, the producer, musical director, choreographer and, possibly, the stage manager should give their notes to the cast, pointing out the weak spots and the parts that need special attention as well as giving praise where it is due. Questions from the company should be resolved there and then where possible, or noted for attention at an early rehearsal. A meeting of the production team and the stage staff to go over notes and formulate the plan of campaign for phase two of rehearsals usually ends the rehearsal.

THE POLISHING STAGE

On a personal note, here is a plea to producers. Too often the amateur musical production reaches this stage and stops. It appears that, if the principals and chorus know their words, music and moves, then the producer is satisfied and the show is presented to the public. But, as a producer, we have barely started work. All we have done so far is to rough out the show – the really interesting aspect of production starts now with the next phase of our rehearsals – the polishing stage. Few amateur musical companies allow sufficient time for this all-important aspect of rehearsals and I believe the fault lies with the producer who allows the blocking rehearsals to prolong indefinitely. He should stipulate early that on a certain date the entire company should be ready for the first run-through rehearsal. Thereafter he should concentrate on the polishing process.

Polishing a show involves questions of meaning, cadence or inflection, vocal quality, response, enunciation as well as ironing out the difficulties inherent in playing love scenes, eating on the stage and similar situations.

Understanding the lines We must assume that, by this stage, the principals have got a good grasp of their lines but there may still be some lack of understanding of them. This should be remedied as soon as possible, and a method frequently recommended and one which I use myself, is to question the artist repeatedly on any points of interpretation of which he appears to be doubtful: Is this line important for the audience? Has it a double meaning? Does it refer back to something already discussed? Is it a laugh line? To whom is it particularly directed? Does it require an answer? And so forth. Sometimes it may be necessary to ask the actor to put the line into his own words to see if he really has grasped its meaning.

The question of which word to emphasize in a line often requires analysis. Consider the variations that can be drawn from this single line from *The Gipsy Baron*.

'You were expecting him?'

1 *You* were expecting him? (of all the others present, you alone)
2 You *were* expecting him? (I did not think you were)
3 You were *expecting* him? (you were anticipating his arrival)
4 You were expecting *him*? (I thought it was somebody else)

The actor must be encouraged to experiment with his lines and the stresses he places on the words to discover for himself the most apt meaning of them.

Pace The producer must also pay particular attention to the speed of dialogue delivery. Most amateurs drag their lines, either because they have memorized them inadequately or because they pick up cues too slowly. I often have a word rehearsal at this stage when I allow the principals to play a scene – at top speed, without any consideration of meaning or movement. A couple of times through a scene works wonders on cue take-up, and the producer can illustrate how much more effective the planned pauses become in contrast.

Amateurs often find trouble with the incomplete sentence, the ones that end . . . They deliver the line exactly as written and however well the cue is taken up, the flow of dialogue appears jerky. The actor should continue the sense of the sentence and allow himself to be actually interrupted.

Whilst aiming for an overall pace, the producer must be wary of letting the individual players pick up each other's speed. Impress upon each character that he or she has a speed of delivery which must accord with the character being portrayed.

Inflections are possibly easier to explain to members of a musical company since one can draw illustrations from music itself. A sentence can be likened to a tune, starting on either an upward or downward scale, delivered in a series of long smooth *legato* phrases or in short *staccato* snatches. *Crescendo* and *diminuendo* are terms which can be used to illustrate the effect that the producer seeks.

Long speeches often need to be broken up. Suitable business can be devised or variations of tempo and facial expression introduced. Above all, the imagination of the actor must be brought into play and must be stimulated constantly by the producer. Questioning the actor about his thoughts and reactions in the given situation certainly helps in this direction.

Love scenes Love scenes are often a source of embarrassment both to the actors and to the audience. They should be carefully rehearsed until the actors are thoroughly certain of their words and movements. Guard against stiff rigid poses and encourage the players to act boldly and, above all, sincerely. Beware of the stereotyped poses so often witnessed in love duets, the pair facing each other clumsily grasping each other's hands. It is far more satisfactory for the girl to stand in front and a little to one side of the man, so that her head appears to rest on his shoulder. His arms can lightly clasp her, taking care not to constrict her diaphragm, and both can sing out to the audience, and not, as so often happens, into each other's faces and the wings. Kisses too present a problem and again thorough rehearsal is called for, care should be taken to avoid an ungainly or ugly posture.

Pronunciation and dialect A problem that frequently arises is that of pronunciation and dialect. I do not think it advisable to be too pedantic on the matter of pronunciation and in any case few producers have the time or the ability to give tuition in voice and diction. Any marked peculiarity of pronunciation should be suppressed unless it is of use to the character being portrayed, and any laziness in pronunciation should be checked. When unfamiliar names of persons or places occur, the producer should seek advice on the accepted pronunciation of these and ensure that all his cast use the agreed pronunciation.

Musicals may be set in a variety of countries: America, France, Ireland, Hungary, Austria, Japan and so on. The question arises whether one should play the show in the dialect of the country concerned, and here I would say emphatically 'No'! Certain principals may give a suggestion of the appropriate dialect to their lines – very often it assists in the characterization, but to allow all and sundry to speak with a stage American dialect in *Oklahoma* or with a French accent in *The Three Musketeers* is to court disaster. My advice is to use dialects rarely, carefully and with restraint, picking out the most suggestive features, and avoiding any exaggeration of them by the cast.

POLISHING THE MUSIC

The chorus work will require tightening up, and whilst the producer is engaged with the principals, the musical director can give them a refresher course on the music. The standard of singing and vocal interpretation invariably falls during the blocking rehearsals, but once the chorus have learned their moves and business of the various ensembles, attention can be directed once more to the vocal side of the production.

The first things to check are the vocal lines of the inner parts of the chorus: the second sopranos, contraltos and baritones. A good attack, and correct note valuation should be checked, particular attention being paid to the final chords of an ensemble to ensure that all the singers come off a note together.

Diction will need to be checked and slovenliness eradicated, whilst every member of the chorus should be encouraged to listen to those about him in order to appreciate a sense of vocal balance. Particular points to watch for are the final consonants, the 'd's, 't's and 'n's and the lingering 's'. One musical director I know teaches his chorus to slightly open the mouth again after singing an 's', thus cutting out any suggestion of the hiss so often heard in amateur chorus work.

The singers should be encouraged to think about the words they are singing. Questioning, similar to the technique used with the principals, will help: Is this a happy song? Are you scolding somebody? To whom are these lines addressed?

Musical directors often have to remind the chorus to watch his stick but the producer must check any tendency by the chorus to stare at the musical director. A demonstration will show the ensemble that it is possible to see the conductor and his cues out of the corner of the eye, without obviously staring. A cue should be anticipated, and the actor should position himself in such a way as to be able to see it easily, without appearing to be obviously looking for it.

CONTINUITY

After the refresher courses, the show can be put together again. Now the producer should play for continuity, aiming to achieve an overall balance and ensuring that the production moves smoothly forward to the final climax. At these rehearsals, interruptions should be avoided and any remarks reserved until the end of each act. It is good practice to devote a session to each act in turn. All properties, or substitutes, should be used and the stage manager should note any variations in the playing time. Comments should be made at the end of the act, and, if time allows, the act played through a second time. At this stage the singers should be encouraged to limber up vocally before rehearsals start. No professional singer would attempt to sing a role without first exercising his vocal cords and this practice will have a salutory effect on all the chorus members.

Amateur choruses often tend to drop out of character when they are not actively engaged on the stage, and the producer should constantly check the reaction of the ensemble when it is present in a scene involving dialogue between principals. Reaction will be seen chiefly on the face, and fidgeting gestures that may tend to distract the audience's attention from the central actor must be discouraged. Here again the questioning technique can be used to advantage to stimulate the imagination of the chorus member. Beware of allowing all the ladies to act as bright young girls or the men as young lads. Nearly every chorus can, with advantage, be made up of all ages and types and the individual should be encouraged to think out a character appropriate to the subject, setting and period of the show.

To sum up briefly on the polishing stage:

1 Test your stage pictures from all angles, bearing in mind the sight-lines. Squint at them, as John Dolman Jnr says
2 Watch rehearsals from far back and from all parts of the auditorium, checking for audibility and visibility
3 Watch for any stiff or unnatural moves. Find out why they appear so, and amend accordingly. Seek to simplify whenever possible
4 Make certain that the significant lines, the plot, are coming across
5 Make certain that each act opens and closes with enthusiasm!
6 Be certain that your actors fully understand the meaning of their lines
7 Watch the speed of the dialogue and check any tendency to drag
8 See that the actors do not pick up each other's speed of delivery
9 Watch for any long speeches that require breaking down
10 Study the playing of love scenes
11 Suppress any tendency to overplay a dialect
12 Teach the actors how to play laughs and take applause
13 Watch the chorus reactions and ensure that they support the central theme
14 Encourage the effect of 'for the first time'.

6 Rehearsals · the final phase and dress rehearsals

'It's curtain time and away we go!'
KISS ME KATE

INTRODUCTION

Bar the usual troubles that so often beset even the best organized amateur companies – sickness, change of cast and members falling by the wayside – the show should be falling into place about two weeks before the opening night and rehearsals must now be devoted to running through the entire show. It may be objected that the company will become stale through constant repetition, but I have yet to see an amateur musical company that showed signs of over-rehearsal. Unhappily the reverse is only too apparent! There is, however, the danger that the members, particularly the chorus, may become bored. To counteract this, the producer should concentrate on a definite aspect at each rehearsal – at one rehearsal he may pay particular attention to diction; at another he may stress the need for playing to the focal point, or, again, he may run the show concentrating on speed and attack. Above all, he must be at his most enthusiastic. So long as the company do not feel that the rehearsal is just another run-through, its interest will not pall.

THE LAST REHEARSALS
The full company is called for these final stages, and the rehearsal should proceed uninterrupted – any notes being given at the end of the evening. Control of rehearsals now comes under the stage manager and matters organized to simulate, as nearly as possible, the conditions of a performance. Any scene changes should be handled by the stage crew – even if this means that they merely go through the motions. Properties should, by now, be used as a matter of course. Any special ones such as swords, rifles and similar accoutrements which are frequently called for in many of the old musicals, should be hired for these last few rehearsals so that the cast become accustomed to handling them.

It is useful to play before a small audience at this stage of rehearsals and honorary or associate members can be invited to attend. Although the show will lack the colour and spectacle afforded by the costumes, settings and lighting, the rehearsals should prove entertaining to your visitors, whilst the company will gain confidence and practice from playing to an audience.

These final rehearsals should be devoted to the cultivation of smoothness. If time does not allow for a period of analysis at the end, the producer and musical director may write out their notes for each principal to study before the next rehearsal. If the company is an experienced one, it is possible to shout one's remarks without interrupting the playing. 'Watch that straight line!' or 'Use all the stage!' the producer may shout to his chorus, or 'Poor exit – carry on!' to a principal. This method is akin to the conductor's remarks at a band call, and, if the company is experienced, they will register the criticism and amend accordingly at the next run-through. What is more, once they have become accustomed to this method, they should be able to keep in character whilst mentally noting the producer's instructions and there should be no loss of smoothness.

Inevitably there will be troublesome scenes but these should be rehearsed separately. Even when a show is developing well, one may have an off night and on such occasions I have found it useful to give the company its head, and let them 'send up' the whole production. The tension is relaxed and the next rehearsal goes with a swing. Moreover, one sometimes finds an actor, particularly among the chorus members, who has devised a bit of business ideally suited to the production, but who has been far too nervous to use it before.

Each scene should be timed and checked against the target times. Generally the show will tend to run faster with succeeding rehearsals and final target times will need to be amended. Any erratic timing requires to be investigated in order to discover the cause and correct it. The various heads of departments, the stage manager, electrician, and effects man can check their cue sheets and proposed lighting intensities during these rehearsals, timing the changes and amending them where necessary.

This pre-planning is of vital importance, particularly to the amateur company. Whilst the professional company will often have a week or more in the theatre prior to the opening night in which to get in, set up the stage and for lighting, orchestral and full rehearsals, the amateur has, all too often, to condense all this work into a weekend. Indeed, the stage is often not available until the close of the Saturday evening performance and one is expected to be ready to open on Monday night! As most amateurs have to do other jobs during the day, one is virtually limited to Saturday night and all day Sunday for this vast operation.

THE ORCHESTRA: SOME REMARKS BY SYDNEY LOCKERMAN

The orchestra is one of the most vital components in a musical. Bad playing, lack of pit discipline and the work of many months could be wrecked at the first performance. If an amateur orchestra is used, the greatest care should be shown in selecting the instrumentalists. Selection by audition is the best method but, whilst there are some good amateur players, I do not recommend using an amateur orchestra. Too much is at stake. Professional and semi-professional musicians are the answer. With the limited time allowed for an orchestra rehearsal (three hours) their technique, discipline and experience are invaluable. The musical director must establish a close relationship with his players so the week of the show becomes an enjoyable experience. If the musical director states what he wants, gives a clear beat, and shows he knows the score, the musicians will respect him and give him their absolute co-operation. A good leader is an absolute must – the right arm of the musical director. Such details as bowing can be discussed and it is useful for the leader to attend a run-through of the show before the orchestra rehearsal.

As regards the orchestra, the firm issuing the band parts should be contacted to find out for which instruments the show is scored. From this information the musical director is able to adjust the number of instruments to fit into his budget – always allowing for the fact that the music must not suffer for the sake of economy.

The size of the theatre, whether there is an orchestra pit and acoustics must all be taken into account. For shows such as *The Merry Widow, White Horse Inn, The Gipsy Baron, Pink Champagne* I have used an orchestra made up as follows: four 1st violins, two 2nd violins, one viola, one 'cello, one bass, one harp, one flute, one oboe, 1st and 2nd clarinet, one horn, 1st and 2nd trumpet, one trombone and percussion. For other shows I have added a bassoon and 2nd trombone. Certain scores are cross-cued which enables the musical director to dispense with the last named instruments, not from choice but from the expense angle. I always mark in *every* band part changes of beat, tempo, cuts and any other adjustments to save time at the orchestra rehearsal. As this rehearsal is only three hours in duration it is essential to *play* for that length of time and not waste it by the musicians marking their own scores. I usually start marking five or six weeks before the orchestra rehearsal which allows time to check any misprints or errors in notation. It must be emphasized that all markings should be made with a soft pencil and erased immediately after the last performance as it is both unfair to the copyright holders to damage their scores by using a ball-point pen or red ink, and to the people who will next be using these scores.

THE BAND CALL

The band call is, of course, primarily for the musical director and the orchestra. In the short time available they have to play right through the score, checking any wrong notes and agreeing the various *tempi*, as well as giving attention to interpretation and style. With their experience, professional players can usually take this in their stride.

Before each number the musical director will clarify such points as number of verses and choruses to be played, cuts (if any) to be observed, which repeats to ignore and whether any encore will be given. He should also state how many beats to the bar will be given (for example, a piece of music written in 3:4 time can be beaten either in three beats or in one beat).

Even with a fully professional orchestra, there are occasions when a new or unfamiliar show is being produced, when more than the single band call will be necessary. The musical director can ascertain this from his earlier studies of the conductor's score.

Some conductors like the cast, or at least the principal vocalists, to attend the band call. Whilst his attention will be directed chiefly to his players, the singers can nevertheless try out their numbers with the orchestra. Unless they are very experienced, they will find, initially, that the score falls strangely on their ears after being so long accustomed to the piano accompaniment. Any vocal problems should not be allowed to intrude on this rehearsal, but dealt with by the musical director at the end of the session. It is not uncommon for the music to be taken at a slightly slower tempo at band call, but the tension and excitement of a performance will soon lift it to its faster tempo.

The arrangement of the players in the orchestra pit varies with individual musical directors. Factors affecting the positioning of the various instruments include the size and shape of the pit, the height of the stage and the instruments for which the show is scored. Consideration must be given to the comfort of the players and adequate space must be allowed to the string players for their bowing and the trombones for their slides. When a piano is called for it is generally situated in the centre of the pit whilst the larger instruments, such as the harp and double bass, which may obstruct the audience's view of the stage, are situated at the extremities. Often no orchestra pit exists and the players are seated on the same level as the audience. In this case, care must be taken to see that the players and their desks offer as little interference as possible with the view of the stage.

The decision on the seating of the orchestra is the musical director's and he should provide the stage manager with a sketch of his requirements so that the pit may be prepared in advance of the band call or the dress rehearsal. In addition he should settle the question of cue lights: whether they are required and what method of signalling should be employed.

If a piano is used on stage during the performance, the stage manager should arrange for it to be tuned to concert pitch for the dress rehearsal, and probably once or twice during the run of the show to ensure that it keeps in tune. Similarly, if a piano is used in the orchestra pit, it will need attention.

THE GET-IN

The stage manager should utilize every moment that the theatre is available to him. In the case of a weekend get-in, he may be able to arrange with the theatre management to allow him to off-load his scenery, properties, wardrobe and lighting equipment into the loading dock on the Saturday morning. Indeed, some managements will allow the band call to be held in the theatre despite another company being in residence. It pays to cultivate the goodwill and co-operation of the resident stage manager and electrician who can often be persuaded to start rigging during the week prior to the performances when circumstances permit. This saves considerable time and can often be the means of getting a satisfactory lighting and setting rehearsal.

When the time arrives for the theatre to be completely turned over to the company, the stage crew, under the direction of the stage manager, swing into action.

48

1 *Kismet* Alfred Drake and Doretta Morrow sing 'Rhymes have I' in this Eastern extravaganza based on the music of Borodin. STOLL THEATRE, LONDON 1955.
Photo: Houston Rogers

2 *The Merry Widow* Margaret Mitchell as the Widow and Colin Thomas as Camille in Jack Hylton's production. STOLL THEATRE, LONDON 1952. *Photo: George J. Keen*

3 *Paint Your Wagon*   Bobby Howes as Ben Rumson in a show that demands a strong male chorus. HER MAJESTY'S THEATRE, LONDON 1953. *Photo: Houston Rogers*

4 *Kiss Me Kate*   An opening chorus making good use of a bare stage. Adelaide Hall as Hattie in 'Another opening, another show'. LONDON COLISEUM 1951. *Photo: Houston Rogers*

5   *The Dancing Years*   A photograph taken during an actual performance of Tom Arnold's production when on tour in 1960.   *Photo: By permission of Tom Arnold*

6   *My Fair Lady*   'Outside the Opera House, Covent Garden on a cold March night –
the opening scene of one of the most famous musical shows. Rex Harrison as Henry
Higgins and Julie Andrews as Eliza Doolittle. THEATRE ROYAL, DRURY LANE,
LONDON 1958.   *Photo: Angus MacBean*

7 *Camelot* Laurence Harvey as Arthur and Elizabeth Larner as Guenevere in the musical version of the Arthurian legend. THEATRE ROYAL, DRURY LANE, LONDON 1964. *Photo: Press Association*

8 *Hello Dolly* Mary Martin, as Dolly, sets off for New York. THEATRE ROYAL, DRURY LANE, LONDON 1965. *Photo: Press Association*

9 *Stop the World – I Want to Get Off* Anthony Newley as Littlechap and Anna Quayle as Evie in a musical requiring only a company of twelve and a single all-purpose set. QUEEN'S THEATRE, LONDON 1961. *Photo: Keystone Press*

If all the preliminary work has been thoroughly planned the work should go smoothly and without mishap. Methods will vary in different companies, but a brief look at a typical get-in may be of interest. One thing that I insist upon is that all tabs, borders and legs that are not required are flown or, if their lines are needed or if there is insufficient head room, they are taken down, packed, labelled and stored until the end of the show. Any other equipment or scenery belonging to the theatre which is not needed should be neatly packed away, so that the stage is as clear as possible.

Then the cloths, borders, trailers and legs used in the show are hung on pre-determined lines. At the risk of stating the obvious, may I point out that all cloths and borders should have their centres marked – usually with a tie of distinctive colour. If no mark can be found, the canvas should be folded, end to end and the centre top determined. This is tied onto the batten directly under the centre flying line. The piece is then hung, working outwards from the middle. This ensures that the cloth or border hangs centrally.

Once all flown pieces and lanterns have been rigged, the set pieces built up and the electrical circuits connected, the stage can be cleared and swept. All old stage markings should be washed out, and if the floats are to be used, clean them also. They are terrible dust traps, and dirty reflectors will cut down their efficiency.

SETTING THE STAGE

Setting can now begin. I have frequently found it a good plan to set the show in reverse, starting with the last scene and working backwards to finish with Act 1 scene 1 standing. The packs of scenery will then be in their correct order, and if time does not allow for a setting rehearsal (as opposed to simply setting and marking which we are discussing) the stage will be ready for the dress rehearsal.

Once the scene is set, the stage manager and the producer should check it from all parts of the house. Check the sight-lines, the masking of openings, make certain that borders and cloths are level and indicate the 'dead' on each flown piece. Once both are satisfied, mark the set and dress it.

Marking the set involves two operations. The position of the scenery is indicated on the floor. This is done discreetly at the important points – angles, ends of runs and so on – with a touch of water-colour. Often a different colour is used for each set. The marks need only be big enough to guide the stage crew when they are positioning flats, and the stage floor need not look like a crazy street guide. The flats too are marked with the act, the scene and the number of the flat. Numbering starts at the DOP side and works around the stage to the DPS.

Dressing the set involves placing or fixing all the furniture, drapes, pictures, door furniture and other properties, including any decorative lighting fittings. Again these should be checked, and once their placing is agreed, their positions marked and noted by the property master.

Finally the scene can be lit. At this point it is well to position the set with actors, since I find that without them one has a tendency to underlight the scene. When the producer is satisfied, the electrician marks his cue sheet with the final levels of lanterns, and if lighting changes are involved, moves on to his next cue.

Once all cues are completed to the satisfaction of the producer, the scene is struck and work proceeds along the same lines to the penultimate scene. Working steadily to this pattern, all the scenes are set, approved and marked.

SETTING REHEARSALS

Now, if time allows, the stage manager and electrician hold a setting rehearsal.

This time the show is taken in its correct sequence, the various tasks involved in a scene change are apportioned and the stage crew work against the clock, attempting to get each change completed in the allocated time. If, as sometimes happens, this proves impractical, the producer and stage manager will need to find a way to resolve the problem. A trailer closed thirty seconds earlier, leaving the soloist to finish a scene in a spotlight on the forestage, may provide the answer or, at worst, extra curtain music must be added to cover the change. There is no hard and fast rule to help the producer find the solution, but some means has to be devised to prevent the audience being left silently watching the curtain.

THE COSTUME PARADE

While the stage manager takes his setting rehearsal, the producer, with the wardrobe mistress, can turn his attention to the costumes. The easiest way to tackle this chore is to hold a costume parade. Often the principals will have been for a fitting and in any case they can be dealt with separately. It is the chorus that need attention, and, again it saves time to see them, in sets, starting with their finale costumes and working backwards through their various changes. Try to see the chorus sets as a whole group. Check that fit, skirt lengths, hair styles, and accessories are correct. If the costume plots have been well made out only minor alterations will be needed and these can be carried out there and then by the seamstresses. Sometimes costumes can be switched about so that everyone has one that is a reasonable fit, but failing this, the offending costume must go back to the hirers with details of the correct size required. Dresses may require pressing: again, the wardrobe mistress's assistants handle this chore, which must be done in the place set aside and authorized by the theatre management.

THE PHOTO-CALL

A brief word here about the photo-call. Amateurs rarely have time to hold a full-fledged photo-call, and such photographs as are required are usually taken as and when possible during the dress rehearsal. Luckily there are photographers who specialize in this. But where time permits, a proper photo-call should be arranged. The photographer can, with the producer, decide on which parts of the show will give the best shots and a programme can be drawn up advising which artists will be required. The pictures do not have to be composed exactly as they are performed in the show and the producer should be advised by the photographer if the latter is an expert. Lighting will have to be modified and the electrician will need to be in attendance. Where time is short, I have obtained good photographs by using the following method. Suitable flats are erected in another part of the theatre whilst the stage is occupied with the rigging crew. Stand floodlights and spots are connected up and the photographer poses and photographs pre-arranged groups during the early part of the 'get-in' day.

THE DRESS REHEARSALS

Finally, the time approaches for the dress rehearsal. I strongly believe that, with adequate pre-planning, a successful dress rehearsal can be undertaken in three hours. Indeed, apart from a handful of exceptions, this is all the time I have ever had at my disposal for the actual rehearsal for the past twelve years. If the show is a new or a particularly difficult one technically, the first dress rehearsal should be played with piano accompaniment only. In this case, the producer can concentrate on technical details and stop where necessary to correct or sort out a difficulty. Normally, however, the dress rehearsal is a trial performance and interruptions are kept to the minimum. Side-line coaching, as mentioned during the earlier part of this chapter, can still be indulged in, but let the performance go through to the end, saving all the criticism until then. Once the performance is over, let the musical director go over any musical problems first of all, so that the orchestra is not kept unduly. Then cover any major faults that may need re-running and finally give notes of any minor faults. Try to dismiss the company at a reasonable hour and, above all, send them home with a feeling of achievement and determination to do better on the night. I certainly do not believe the old saying that a bad dress rehearsal means a good show. With nervousness and the strangeness of their surroundings minor mishaps are unavoidable but, if the show has major faults at this stage, the fault lies with the producer.

7 Sets and settings

'Pretty things, where is the girl who can resist them?'
ROSE MARIE

INTRODUCTION

Forty years ago *The Desert Song* had its première and, as I write this book, it is again drawing large houses at London's Palace theatre. *The Desert Song* is one of the earliest successful musicals and John Hanson's revival employs the same staging methods that were current in 1927. Even so, techniques of mounting musicals have undergone some revolutionary changes over the past decade.

Initially musicals were written in two, three or four acts, each act comprising one set. Box sets were used for interiors and wings and borders for the exteriors. Scene changes were made in the intervals and hidden from the audience by the house curtain. *The Vagabond King, Lilac Time, The Quaker Girl* and the Savoy Operas fall into this category.

In the 1930's a musical production meant a spectacle. *White Horse Inn* introduced on to the stage a lake steamer, assorted live animals and a torrential thunderstorm; it made use of revolves and included an orchestra of over one hundred musicians. In this type of production the acts are now broken down into a variety of different scenes. These alternate between full stage settings and front cloths. They continued to be played in the proscenium picture stage setting and, to facilitate rapid scene changes, much use was made of flown cloths, cut-outs, French flats and trucks apart from the revolving stages already referred to. Scene changes were still masked from the sight of the audience by using trailers or blackouts. Examples of the spectacle would include most of the Ivor Novello shows – *Perchance to Dream, King's Rhapsody* and *The Dancing Years* to name but three.

It was not until the arrival of *West Side Story* and *My Fair Lady* that scene changes actually took place in the sight of the audience. With these productions this aspect of staging became an integral visual part of the show. Music and lighting were used both to cover the changes and to set the mood of the new scene, while the physical handling of much of the scenery was carried out by either dancers or the stage crew in full view of the audience.

It is now quite commonplace for scenery to be changed in front of the audience. Watching the various permutations that were possible with Sean Kelly's clever multi-purpose set was part of the fun of *Oliver*. Also memorable was the automated scenery by the same designer for Lionel Bart's *Blitz*. The elaborate settings used in the West End or Broadway productions become impractical once the show goes on the road, and very often a simplified touring set is designed. It is these settings that are usually hired out to amateur groups.

Since, in recent years, we have seen the demolition of many of the local theatres and music halls which served as homes for the local operatic societies, it is rare to find a company lucky enough to play in a real theatre. We should, however, consider the facilities available in the professional house before proceeding to discuss ways of overcoming the shortcomings of the local town hall or community centre.

Fig. 15 shows an impression of the back-stage area of a proscenium-type stage.

The acting area   The part of the stage on which the actor appears. It should be in clear view from all parts of the auditorium and its area is determined by the seating arrangements in the 'house' and the sight-lines from those seats.

The working area or wing space   The area at the sides of the acting area. It should be large enough to accommodate the packs of flats necessary for scene changes, the furniture, properties and other equipment, as well as allowing space for the chorus to assemble.

The proscenium opening   This is the picture frame through which the audience see the play. It is often referred to as the 'fourth wall'. Very often, a false proscenium is built upstage of this, which serves both as a setting edge for box sets, and, with its adjustable border, a method of masking the top of the scenery.

The prompt corner   By tradition, downstage left, and is usually where the prompter actually sits. It is also the working corner and it is here that the stage manager will have his desk and cue board and from whence he controls the entire running of the show.

Electrician's switchboard   In the older theatres, this is usually erected some eight feet above stage level and is generally on the prompt side, although nowadays, thanks to modern electrical practice, many theatres have a lighting console in a special booth at the back of the auditorium.

The flies   This is the space above the stage where scenery, cloths and drapes are hung when not in use. It gets its name because scenery 'flies up there'.

The grid   This can best be described as a false, skeleton ceiling just under the roof of the stage. In this grid are mounted the blocks and leads, over which the lines that carry the scenery will travel. Each backcloth, drape, or lighting batten will have three lines by which it can be raised or lowered. These lines are called long, centre and short line respectively, the short line being the one nearest to the fly floor. These lines run over blocks on the grid thence to the lead which has three wheels and so down to the fly floor where they can be tied off on a cleat.

The dips   Small traps in the floor of the stage, usually at the edges of the acting area, containing sockets for plugging in various electrical equipment. Very often they are paired across stage.

The carpet cut   This is a small trapdoor just upstage of the front curtain and running the width of the stage. Its purpose is to trap the forward edge of a stage cloth, saving the use of tacks and preventing the actors from tripping up.

It is interesting at this juncture to note the dimensions of one of the large

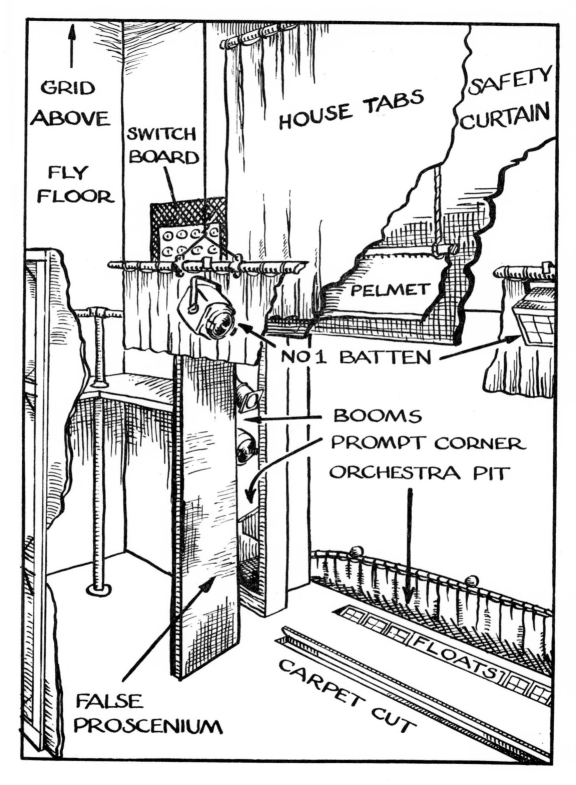

GRID
ABOVE

FLY
FLOOR

SWITCH
BOARD

HOUSE TABS

SAFETY
CURTAIN

PELMET

NO 1 BATTEN

BOOMS
PROMPT CORNER
ORCHESTRA PIT

FLOATS

FALSE
PROSCENIUM

CARPET CUT

FIG 15   An impression of backstage

London stages which has long been the home of the spectacular musical – the Theatre Royal, Drury Lane:

Proscenium width	42 ft	Height of grid from stage	71 ft
Proscenium height	31 ft	Height to flies above stage floor	35 ft
Stage width	79 ft	104 lines	
Stage depth from setting line	78 ft	6 lifts	
Electric console switchboard – 216 ways, each with its own dimmer.			

With all these facilities available, there is rarely a musical at Drury Lane that does not require '. . . additional lighting by . . .' and, if I had suggested no other reasons, this should be enough to convince you that one should not attempt to reproduce the original production. Few, if any, amateur companies can command the talent, facilities and stage space of the professionals and it is, I suggest, far better to envisage a new concept of the piece, tailored to one's local resources.

THE TOWN HALL STAGE

Let us now take a brief look at what we can expect to find at the average community theatre or town hall stage. In the first place the majority of these were never conceived as theatres. It is only of recent date that the idea of local civic theatres gained favour and most amateur companies play in a hall that was designed for a variety of other purposes. Consequently, they must be prepared to contend with a stage of minimal dimensions, usually complete lack of head-room or working space together with rudimentary lighting equipment. There is seldom an orchestra pit, and the auditorium is rarely raked whilst the seating arrangements give trouble with sight-lines.

The producer of amateur musicals must therefore be a master of compromise and adaptation. He should acquaint himself with the layout and facilities of his theatre at a very early date in order that he may resolve the many problems that he will encounter there. A plan of the stage area, drawn to scale and indicating such amenities as exist is essential. It is also useful to have a scaled plan of the theatre and a cross section drawing if one is available. Not until he has these details can he start to consider sets and setting.

SCENERY

The scene design together with all the furniture and fittings, as well as the properties and costumes to be used is really the province of the artistic director who advises and guides the producer on these matters, but since an artistic director is the exception rather than the rule in operatic societies, the producer must, perforce, be able to perform this function as well as his other duties.

The function of scenery It may be argued that scenery is unnecessary and that the performance can be just as effective when played before neutral drapes. Whilst not entirely disagreeing with this premise, I maintain that a musical, in particular, relies on both the visual and the aural impact and, if the visual aspect is missing the performance becomes a concert version or a recital, even if costumes are used.

Let us agree then that scenery is a pre-requisite of a musical production and consider its functions. In 1964 the *Architects' Journal* devoted several issues to a comprehensive coverage of auditoria and stages (volume 140, numbers 2–11, July 8th–September 9th, 1964).

In the technical study devoted to stage scenery the functions were stated as: '. . . to assist the visual expression of the dramatic performance by:

   i Providing a geography for the actor within the stage space;
   ii Painting the action and atmosphere of the play;
   iii Clarifying the time and place of the action'.

It does not matter whether the scenery is starkly symbolic or the most naturalistic, since all scenery is a deception and theatre audiences accept the convention of suspended belief and willingly enter into the spirit of make-believe.

Scenery can be described as being either two-dimensional or three-dimensional. As the description implies, two-dimensional scenery is flat although sometimes several units may be assembled to make a three-dimensional form on the stage. Two-dimensional scenery can be further classified as either framed or unframed and together these groups will account for the majority of scenery used in a musical production – embodying the cloths, borders, legs, flats, wings and stage draperies.

The term three-dimensional scenery is self-explanatory and includes all the solid forms used – rostra, pillars, staircases, rocks, tree stumps and the like. These may be sub-divided into practical and non-practical pieces. Staircases and rostra are examples of practical weight-bearing solids while decorative pillars can be termed non-weight bearing.

It does not fall within the province of this volume to discuss the various methods of constructing and handling scenery although it is an advantage for the producer to have a basic knowledge of these subjects. He should make an effort to familiarize himself with the various scene handling techniques; the comparative advantages and disadvantages of the pin-and-rail and counter-weight systems of flying; bridling; breasting and tripping techniques as well as the functions of tracked and pivoted wagons, revolving stages, lift or elevator stages and the uses of various traps. One of the best publications that I have come across that covers every aspect of this subject is *Scene Design and Stage Lighting* by W. Owen Parker and Harvey K. Smith, published by Holt, Rinehart and Winston.

Ideally, every production should be specially designed for the particular stage on which it is played. The amateur company, however, is left with the choice of either hiring or making their own.

Hiring scenery   This is not simply a question of finding a suitable contractor, agreeing a price and waiting for the delivery of the sets. A great deal of preliminary work must be done before the scenic plots can be finalized. Although most of the past fifty productions that I have staged utilized hired scenery, I have rarely used the sets exactly as they appeared in the original plans submitted by the contractors.

Firms that specialize in hiring scenery for musical productions generally deal in stock sizes – namely 18-foot flats for full size stages and 12-foot flats for smaller halls. They usually supply copies of the settings used in the original professional or touring production and their settings will, more often than not, copy those to be found illustrated in the acting edition libretto of the show. As I have already pointed out, these settings were designed for a specific theatre with all its attendant equipment and resources, and all too often they are quite impractical for the average amateur venue.

However, we need a starting point, and the first thing to be decided is who shall supply the scenery. In most cases there will be a choice of firms able to equip the production and it is as well to know something about their products. A would-

FIG 16   The scenic contractor's plots for *Gipsy Baron*

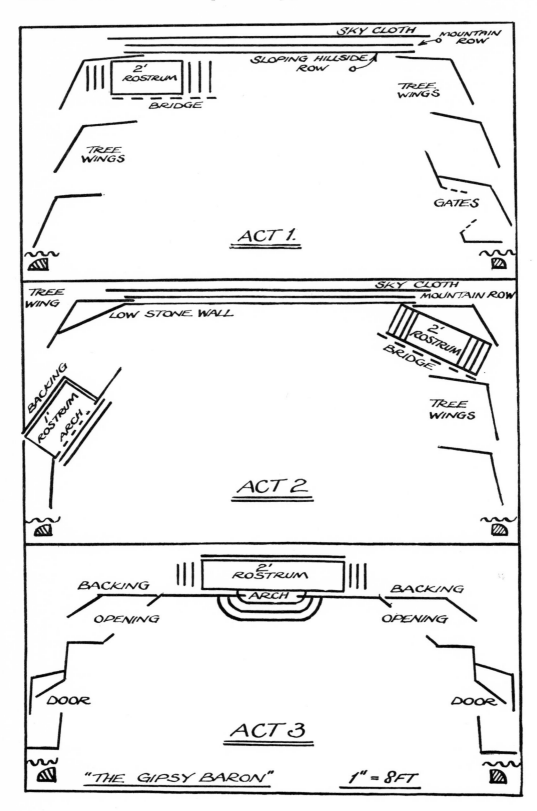

be producer should mark the various settings of any production he may see and particularly any that appeal to him, making special note of the scenic contractor who supplied the sets. Their name should be found in the programme. In this way he will get to know the style and standard of the various studios. Thus Messrs A he finds, paints in analine dyes, and his backcloths tend to be translucent. These are ideal for back lighting, but they do necessitate the use of 'blinders' when used as half stage settings. On the other hand, Messrs B fails to keep his sets in good order, the flats show a tendency to warp and allow light to bleed through and repairs and retouching of paint-work may prove necessary! Quotations should always be sought from a short list of possible suppliers. This is well worth while, since it is not always the firm nearest one's home town whose rates are the cheapest.

Once a contractor has been decided upon, obtain scale plans of the sets he proposes to supply. They will usually look something like those illustrated in fig. 16 which are for a production of *The Gipsy Baron* at a town hall theatre.

Transfer these plans to the scale drawing you have prepared of the stage ($\frac{1}{4}$ inch = 1 foot or $\frac{1}{2}$ inch = 1 foot) and see whether the sets will actually fit the stage. Consider the amount of acting area they give you; check the sight lines; decide what lines you will use to fly the cloths, borders and tab tracks. Check that the entrances are where you require them, that they are wide enough to allow the passage of any large properties that have to be carried on in the course of the action (barrows, market stalls, etc.) as well as allowing for easy movement by the cast. Are they easily changed and can they readily be stored in the wings or scene dock? These are but a few of the matters to be considered and discussed with the stage manager and invariably some amendments are necessary to make the sets fit your requirements.

Usually the cry is for more space: 'How can I get a chorus of thirty-six plus the eight dancers on to that set?' There are ways of making the set look bigger. Exteriors can often benefit by using a plain, well-lit sky cloth and ground rows,

FIG 17   The amended plot for *Gipsy Baron*, Act 3

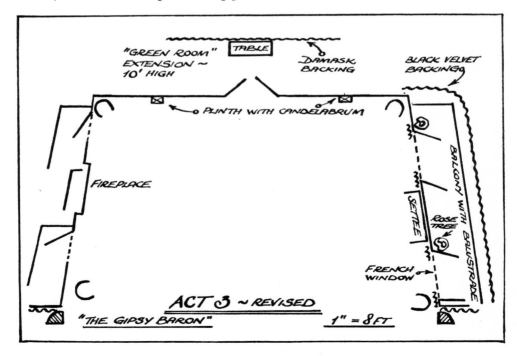

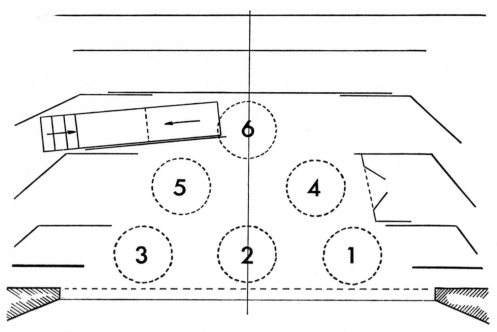

FIG 18   The amended plot for *Gipsy Baron*, Act 1, illustrating the numbering of
lighting areas

rather than a detailed landscape cloth. Wings can be set wider than the proscenium opening – I know that part will not be visible to some sections of the audience, but unless some vital action has to take place near a wing, what does it matter. Even interiors can be re-set to allow more stage space (see fig. 17). If height allows, rostrums can be used, allowing the ensemble to be placed at varying levels. To achieve more depth it may be useful to build out the apron to a greater depth; sometimes, subject to local fire regulations, it is even possible to set some scenery before the proscenium arch.

Adapting hired scenery   To revert to the particular case of *The Gypsy Baron* settings. The contractors knew that the stage in question boasted very few lines suitable for flying cloths. Consequently they proposed a plain sky cloth that could double in both Acts 1 and 2. To get a variation of skyline, various ground rows were proposed (see fig. 18). However, they did not allow for lighting units to be concealed behind these rows in order to bottom light the sky, and to accommodate these lanterns the ground rows had to be plotted at least three feet further downstage. This in turn upset the rest of the setting, which needed to be replotted.

Again, the gates as shown in Act 1 are too far downstage on the PS for the important action that takes place by them. They would not be seen by the audience seated on the extreme right (PS) of the hall as we discovered by plotting the sightlines. To move them on stage here would cut down the stage area, so they had to be moved upstage by eight feet and brought further on stage.

The bridge indicated UR is a main entrance for the chorus and the steps shown would be a notorious source of trouble when a mass entrance or exit is required. A gentle slope was substituted, and a low ramp leading to a two-foot high rostrum served the purpose.

These are not all the difficulties we encountered but I quote them in some detail to show what can be gleaned from a careful study of scaled stage plots, and how time can be saved and frustration averted at the later dress rehearsals.

Sight-lines A word here about sight-lines.

These are the audience's lines of visibility and determine how much of the stage is in view. They can be easily determined mathematically using a sheet of graph paper, a foot-rule, and a plan and elevation of the theatre. The horizontal sight-lines which are drawn from the outer-most seats on the left and right where a member of the audience can be seated, are illustrated on the plan in fig. 19.

The vertical sight-lines are harder to plot since there is seldom a sectional drawing of the theatre available, and they are most difficult when the auditorium comprises one or more balconies. They are plotted as in fig. 20.

The pattern of these sight-lines will determine the shape of the sets and also the acting area where an action will be in full view from all parts of the theatre. Whilst it is often necessary for some, at least, of the ensemble to be hidden from the audience's view, the principal players should always be positioned well within the acting area.

The final scenic plot Our revised settings were drawn up to scale, fully detailed, and returned to the contractors for their comments. Since the firm concerned was close at hand, an appointment was made (NB – always make an appointment!) to discuss the proposed changes. Such meetings are of immense value and I have found that an hour spent with the hirers will result in the whole matter being settled. Moreover, one can usually see specimen flats and get an indication of colour schemes. This is particularly helpful with interior sets when there are furniture and fittings to select elsewhere.

SIGHT-LINES B
1 Stage area   3 Front row end seats
2 Orchestra pit   4 Back row end seats (stalls)
5 Centre of back row of stalls. N.B. If auditorium splays, additional
  sight-lines should be plotted from end seat of widest row

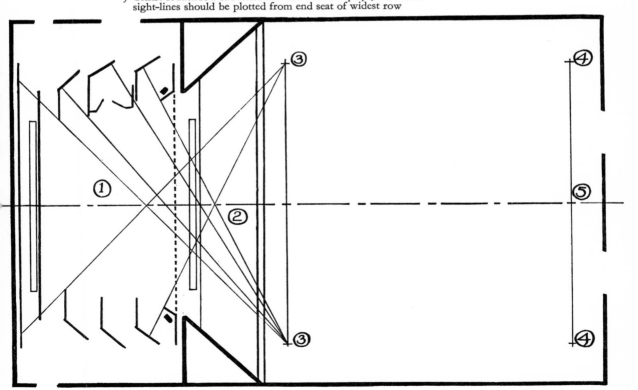

FIG 19 Horizontal sight-lines

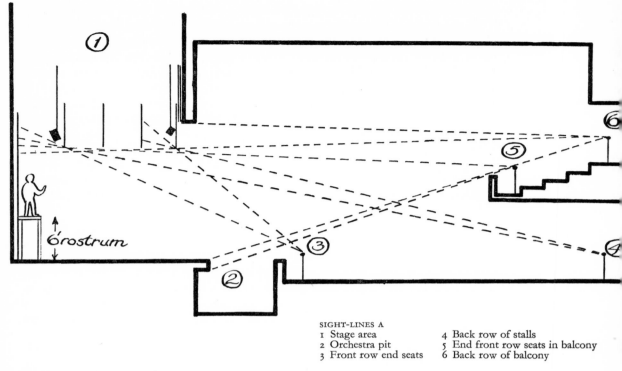

6' rostrum

FIG 20   Vertical sight-lines

When the plots are finalized, detailed scale plans are drawn up and copies sent to the supplying company, the stage manager, producer and choreographer. The last two can then set to work on the book and the dance routines with full knowledge of the dimensions and limitations of the sets.

Still on the subject of scenery hire, it is worth noting that many suppliers will also provide certain properties. This is usually done as a matter of course, but many firms do not indicate what they will provide on their scenic plots and one often ends up with two articles and is involved in needless expense. Under this heading come such items as the roundabout in *Carousel*, the surrey in *Oklahoma* (as well as the basket tree lights!), the trick knife board used in *Pajama Game* apart from such mundane items as tree stumps, benches, rustic tables and trunks. It is well worth while to enquire what the contractor can supply and detail the items on the finalized plot.

Making your own scenery   Recently, more amateur groups are experimenting with sets and costumes of their own design and construction. In the last twelve months I have noted several exciting accounts of such enterprises – among them a production in the round of *West Side Story*; projected scenery used for *Brigadoon* and do-it-yourself sets for *The Land of Smiles*. I have myself experienced the thrill of conceiving a show from scratch with the London amateur première of *The Wizard of Oz* and know how exciting it is to have a show designed to my particular needs. The release to amateurs of shows like *Camelot*, *How to Succeed in Business*, *My Fair Lady* and *Half a Sixpence* provides fruitful material for the imaginative designer and producer alike. Although such a venture is not always cheaper than hiring sets and costumes, the rewards are infinitely greater.

There is neither the space, nor is this the place to explore in depth the questions of the design and construction of scenery and costumes in this book. Many excellent publications exist which go into the subject in exhaustive detail which the director would be well advised to study, and I have listed a few titles in the bibliography at the end of this book.

STAGE PROPERTIES

Simultaneously, with consideration of the various scenic backgrounds involved in a musical production should be discussed the properties. All too often this aspect of the production design is left until late in the rehearsal schedule resulting in poor and unsuitable properties being used. Although most of the firms who specialize in the supply and hire of stage furniture and properties will not reserve items until about a week before the production is staged, the producer should, nevertheless, have a clear idea of his requirements early in the planning stages, and draw up a detailed property plot.

What is a prop? In effect the name embraces every item that is not part of the fixed set together with everything carried or handled by the actors. Sometimes a small piece of scenery becomes a prop, as for example a tree stump or a log, and as such will come under the control of the property master. Properties can be classified under the following headings:

Hand properties   These include small objects actually handled by the actors on the stage. They include letters, books, fans, wine glasses and the like.

Personal properties   When they are peculiar to one individual and are carried by him. Strictly speaking they are costumes: handkerchiefs, quizzing glasses, rings and snuff-boxes would come into this category.

Set properties   These are the larger elements, more closely related to the scenery, but still used by the actors. In this group would come the furniture, tree stumps and stock pieces.

Dress properties   Their function is to complete and dress the set to give it unity. Pictures, window curtains, ornaments and even certain pieces of furniture not specifically used in the action can come under this heading. Strangely enough, all sound and visual effects, apart from electrically powered ones come under the heading of props.

The responsibility for the design or selection of properties should fall to the artistic director, but as few amateur musical companies can boast such a person the job is often delegated to the property master, although I prefer to undertake the selection of properties myself. In any case the final approval of the producer should be sought on all properties used. The producer should have some knowledge of period architecture and decoration, or at least sources of such knowledge to which he can readily refer. This research can be one of the many enjoyable facets of production and I have, on occasions, had to seek advice from the British Museum, the Austrian Embassy, the late W. McQueen Pope and the proprietor of the White Horse Inn at Wolfgansee, to name but a few examples. In every case I found the individuals, whose assistance I sought, to be extremely helpful and co-operative.

When selecting furniture and furnishings, it is essential to know the basic colours of the setting, in order that drapes and upholstery should not jar with the general scheme. Unless the type of production calls for it, one should avoid choosing very bright colours which might clash with the actors costumes and distract the eye to unimportant details. All pieces should be checked for size, suitability and ease of use by the actors.

One should not, for example, select an elbow chair when the actress using it wears a large hooped crinoline. Generally the greatest care has to be exercised when selecting properties for interiors and their visual contribution cannot be over-emphasized. Apart from the points already discussed – the aptness of the piece historically or nationally, one must also consider its rightness for the actual show. 'Is this the kind of furniture that Mr Veit would choose?' 'Are these the curtains that the Grand Duchess Sophie would have selected?' – and so on.

Smaller properties can be obtained or made by the property master. The initial designs should once again be agreed by the producer, who should also approve any items that are bought or hired. One should take extra care over the detail of small properties. If the show calls for an Austrian newspaper – as does *Pink Champagne*, then let it be an Austrian newspaper and not last week's copy of the local scandal sheet. One should go further and attempt to find a newspaper with no visible half-tone photographs (since they were not published at that period!). Letters and documents should contain the actual wording when it is indicated in the script, telegrams and cables should be of the correct size and colour, flowers should be appropriate for the country and the season of the year, and so forth.

Door fittings are seldom supplied by the scenic contractors and the provision of appropriately designed handles and finger-plates can greatly add to the correct appearance of a setting. Electric fittings – wall sconces, candelabra, table lamps and the like are properties and are placed on the set by the property master, although they are connected up and maintained by the electrical department. Care should be exercised in the placing of such items to ensure that they do not mask the actors nor direct distractingly bright light into the eyes of the audience.

For further and more detailed reading of this side of production see the sections on properties, effects and scene construction on p. 123 in the bibliography.

COSTUMES

Finally, in this chapter let us turn to the question of the costumes. As with scenery, the ideal arrangement is to have them specially created for the production in hand, where the costume and stage designers can work in collaboration with the producer to create a unique visual conception of the author's work. However, the majority of amateur productions are dressed by one of the big costumiers who specialize in such work.

Once the show has been decided upon, the company's business manager should obtain a quotation for the hire of the wardrobe. It is important that he gives an indication of the number of actors and dancers involved, since most costumiers work on the original professional production as a basis for their estimates, and the complement of the original company rarely compares with that of an amateur production.

Normally the general management committee will ensure that the wardrobe is available on the dates of their proposed production, and will ask the costumiers to reserve tentatively or pencil-in their dates. The period for which the costumier is prepared to pencil-in a wardrobe depends on a variety of factors, but they rarely like to reserve for longer than a week. It is imperative therefore that the pencil booking is confirmed as soon as possible.

The dates of the *performances* should be given when applying for costumes together with the date of the dress rehearsal or rehearsals. Most hiring firms base their estimates on a schedule of Monday to Saturday performances, with a dress rehearsal on the previous Saturday or Sunday. Any variation to this should be stated when applying for the wardrobe, as it will affect the hiring fee.

Once the society has made a firm booking, the producer comes into the picture, so far as the costumier is concerned. During the early stages of planning his production, he should have formulated his ideas on the costuming of the show. If he decides to follow the original version, more or less, there will be no difficulties, since the costumier will know exactly what costumes should be necessary.

If, however, the producer is creating a new conception of the show, he must consult the costumier at an early stage to see whether his requirements can be met. Unfortunately, far too many societies ignore this point and merely send in their completed measurement forms three or four weeks before their production and are then dismayed when the costumier cannot accede to their particular demands. A spokesman for one of the largest theatrical costumiers told me: 'The ideal method is for the producer, once he has decided how he wishes to dress a show, to contact us and arrange a visit to our premises to discuss the production and, if need be, view costumes.' Bear in mind that the majority of amateur productions are staged between October and early December and during the whole of March, April and early May. Throughout this period costumiers are working round the clock so such visits should be made in the quieter months of the year. I know from experience that such consultations are of immense value and one receives whole-hearted co-operation and assistance from the costumiers.

When all the production details have been settled, the measurement forms should be completed by the wardrobe master/mistress in consultation with the producer. The accurate measuring of the cast is very important, and all the measurements asked for on the forms should be obtained. It is well known that the ladies are sometimes a little difficult on this point, and it has been known for them to give the measurements they would like to be, rather than the measurements they really are. One error that is frequently made is that 'bra' sizes are given instead of 'bust' sizes (there is sometimes a considerable difference!).

Most costumiers have on their measurement forms a note to the effect that 'any outsize measurements should be advised well in advance' as it may not be possible to supply a costume to outsize measurements. It is also important that new measurements are taken for every production.

For the larger productions, where there may be many changes of costume, the details of what is required for *each person in each scene* should be stated. This is very important when the producer's requirements differ from the original estimate. It is quite common for measurement forms to be returned to the costumier completely blank, except for the actual sizes, and this causes a great deal of unnecessary correspondence, time and trouble for both the costumier and the society.

It is the normal practice for the costume hampers to be sent to societies by passenger train. Many societies prefer to use road transport and this should be negotiated separately with the costumiers, who, where they can, will fall in with such arrangements. One important point must be mentioned: where an arrangement has been made that the costumes will be ready for collection at a certain hour on a certain day, it should be adhered to. It will be appreciated that, during the very busy periods of the season mentioned above, every hour is important. A costumier may be sending out between ten and thirty productions in one week, and has to work very strictly to arranged times and dates.

When the costumes are received they should be issued by a responsible person, and any shortage and misfits reported as soon as possible. *The only judge of the suitability of a costume should be the producer under the actual stage conditions.*

Relations between amateur companies and costumiers are not always what they should be, and all too often the fault lies with the amateur. Here, to conclude this chapter, are a few remarks made by a costumier which may give us cause to reflect.

'We now come to one of the main causes of friction between societies and costumiers – the question of make-up on costumes. The sequence of events is as follows: make-up is applied for the dress rehearsal – some of which is left on the costume; a further application of make-up is made for the first performance – some more is left on the costume, and so on throughout the week, with the result that by the time the costumes are returned to the costumier they will have received six or seven layers of make-up; the first layer having been there for eight or nine days, the second layer for seven or eight days and so on; the final result being that the layers of make-up have had varying periods of time to penetrate the fabric. The costumes are cleaned when received by the costumiers, but normal chemical cleaning will only remove the layers of make-up which have not had sufficient time to penetrate the fabric, with the result that there are stains left in the costumes. These can only be removed by washing and boiling the garment. This obviously cannot be done with the majority of costumes due to the nature of the materials, and intensive cleaning processes would reduce the life of the costume considerably.

'It is very difficult to understand why so many amateurs consider it necessary to apply so much make-up and to a much larger area than professionals ever do. Even after a long run in the West End with a possible tour after that run, costumes are not marked to anywhere near the same degree that they are after one week's hire to so many amateur societies. This has been a problem for many years, and no one has yet been able to find a solution.

'Another of the chief causes of stained costumes is the use of "fizzy" drinks to simulate "champagne". These stains cannot be removed and, because of the high cost of costumes, one that has been stained in this way cannot be simply discarded.

'When returning costumes after the production the hampers should be packed as far as possible in the same way as they were received. Great care should be taken to see that hats and fragile head-dresses are not packed in the bottom of hampers under heavy boots or swords, as is too often the case. If any special instructions were included in the hampers when they were received, these should be observed when packing for return.

'Arrangements should have already been made for the return of the hampers by road transport, or by passenger train, and they should be despatched on the next working day after the last performance. It is sometimes not realized that when costumes are returned by British Railways, they will not actually be put on a train until the carriage charges have been paid. It is not sufficient to ask the railway to collect the hampers. This will be done, but the goods will not be despatched until the carriage has been paid.

1 Circumference of head

2 Forehead to poll

3 Ear to ear – measured across the forehead

4 Ear to ear – measured across top of the head

5 Temple to temple – measured round the back of head

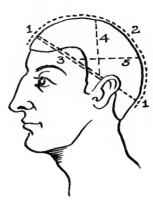

FIG 21   Measurements required for a wig

10 *Music Man* Nan Munro in a spoof on the Statue of Liberty. ADELPHI THEATRE, LONDON 1961. *Photo: Keystone Press*

11 *Bye Bye Birdie* An unusual setting for a chorus number which satirised the telephone habits of the modern teenager. HER MAJESTY'S THEATRE, LONDON 1961. *Photo: Keystone Press*

12

13

12 *Robert and Elizabeth* June Bronhill as Elizabeth Barrett and Keith Michell as Robert Browning in the musical version of *The Barretts of Wimpole Street*. LYRIC THEATRE, LONDON 1964. *Photo: Keystone Press*

13 *Pickwick* Harry Secombe in the title role. SAVILLE THEATRE, LONDON 1963. *Photo: Press Association*

14 *Oliver!* Martin Stephens, as Oliver, asks Mr Bumble (Paul Whitsun-Jones) for more. During the long run of this show the boys were constantly growing out of their parts and had to be replaced. NEW THEATRE, LONDON 1960. *Photo: Anthony Crickmay*

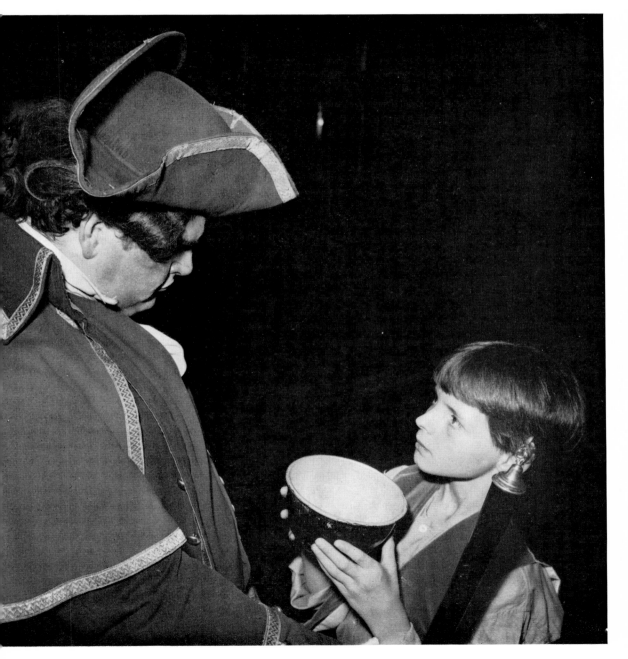

16 *Jorrocks*   Joss Ackland, in the title role, returns to his tea warehouse in the City, in the opening scene of the musical based on the Surtees' stories. NEW THEATRE, LONDON 1966.   *Photo: Anthony Crickmay*

17 *Fiddler on the Roof* – 'The Bottle Dance' from the London production which introduced actor Topol to English audiences. HER MAJESTY'S THEATRE, LONDON 1967.   *Photo: Zoë Dominique*

18   *Baker Street*   Fritz Weaver as Sherlock Holmes and Inge Swenson as his lady love in a musical based on the life and adventures of the great detective. Never produced professionally in England, this show is now available to amateur companies. BROADWAY THEATRE, NEW YORK 1963.   *Photo: Keystone Press*

19 *Lock Up Your Daughters* Bernard Miles and Hy Hazel as Mr and Mrs Squeezum with Sally Smith as Hilaret. MERMAID THEATRE, LONDON 1962. *Photo: Press Association*

'The hiring fee for costumes ranges from 27/6d each to £5.5 each, which would appear to be quite reasonable when it is considered that costs are continually rising. Consider these examples of the current costs for items that go to make up a complete costume:

Boots as worn with Hussar uniforms – £12.12 per pair
Gown for Lord Chancellor in *Iolanthe* – £1,200
Judge's wig   – £45 (takes four years to deliver)
Laundering for one set of dress linen – 10/6d

'The greatest possible care should always be taken of costumes when in the possession of societies. Remember, after your production they have to be cleaned and prepared for another company!'

8 The stage staff

'Life upon the wicked stage'
SHOW BOAT

INTRODUCTION

Any theatrical production is a team effort and a musical production involves a larger team than the straight play. I have already discussed the roles and contributions made by the musical director and the choreographer, and now I want to consider the duties of the rest of the team.

The territory beyond the footlights is the realm of the stage manager. Everything that takes place backstage and every person engaged in the theatre is subject to him. The producer has over-riding control, but he invariably works through the stage manager.

One hears of occasions when the producer is his own stage manager, or when the stage manager actually takes part in the performance. These practices are deplored, since both the producer and the stage manager have their individual jobs to perform whilst rehearsals are in progress as well as during the running of a performance and their efforts should be confined to these duties. In an emergency, a producer may play a role at short notice – it is often more convenient to do this than to do a crash training programme with someone else – but this should be the exception rather than the rule.

THE STAGE MANAGER

Without a doubt, the stage manager is the producer's right-hand man. A stage manager needs to be a man of many parts and a devotee of the theatre. It is an asset if he has had some experience of amateur acting and he must certainly be familiar with the mechanics of the stage. His duties are legion. He should work hand-in-glove with the producer from the earliest inception of the production until the 'get-out' after the final performance. He will have a lot of detail work to do, and must therefore be a methodical and painstaking individual. The preparation of the master prompt-book, the scenic, lighting, property and furniture plots, the various cue sheets and call sheets are his responsibility. During the actual running of the show, he will be in complete control backstage and he needs to be a person capable of making quick decisions. Add to all these duties, the qualities of a tactful personality, a sense of drive and the ability to control. Quite a lot to ask of one man, and the good stage manager will also have the ability to delegate. His job is not made any easier by the fact that, for one reason or another, the amateur company can rarely command the facilities that are available to the professional theatre. Consequently, one of the amateur stage manager's greatest assets is the ability to improvise.

In the early stages of production, the stage manager will collaborate with the producer on matters of scenery, costumes, properties and additional lighting, and it is he who will order these, arrange for their delivery and see that they are returned after the show. Even more than the producer, he needs to have a good working knowledge of scenery construction and painting techniques; on the erection and rigging of all manner of sets; on the functions of various stage lanterns and how they are rigged so that he can advise and guide the producer on these matters. In *The Pan Book of Amateur Dramatics*, Alan Wykes aptly summed up the role of the stage manager: 'The stage manager's job is a creative one; but he is a creator in the practical rather than the abstract sense.'

THE PROMPT COPY

We have already considered, in detail, the preparation of the producer's script in chapter 2. The stage manager's version is basically the same. During rehearsals, either he or the assistant stage manager will record any changes or additions decided by the producer and it is this copy that becomes the official version of the show. It will contain details of the settings, the entrances, exits and business of the actors, as well as the various cues for lighting, curtains, music, effects and any other details necessary for the smooth running of the show. Much of this information can be copied from the producer's script, but the stage manager's version will embody much more detail. For example, the producer's copy may merely state that a scene opens in broad daylight. The stage manager's version will give precise details of which electrical circuits are involved, the level of the various dimmers and the colour filters used. Similar explicit details will be noted regarding the properties, furniture, settings and effects.

THE ASSISTANT STAGE MANAGER

To assist him in his work the stage manager may have one or more assistant stage managers. They do not need to be as experienced as the stage manager and the job is frequently undertaken by women. Enthusiasm and utter dependability are the requisites. In a large-scale production it is often desirable to have an assistant stage manager in control of each side of the stage, working directly under the stage manager who controls the show from the prompt corner.

THE ELECTRICIAN

This functionary will be discussed in the introductory paragraph of the chapter on lighting. In most cases the hall or theatre will have its own resident electrician, but it is usual for the company to provide one also, and he will work with the resident technician, under the direct control of the stage manager. A complicated lighting plot may well require an additional switchboard necessitating two or more operators. In addition, assistants will be required to operate the FOH follow-spots, and to handle the lanterns used on the stage.

THE PROPERTY MASTER

The property master is responsible for all the furniture and properties used in the production. He often has one or two assistants, depending on how complicated the show is, and in such a case, will delegate one to each side of the stage. A property master needs to be an expert scrounger and an inveterate hoarder. If, on occasion, he cannot beg, borrow or steal the necessary prop, he must be able to make it. The property plot should contain details of the property, its position on the stage (indicated on a sketch plan) for whom the property is intended, and from where it was obtained (see fig. 22). The last detail is important, and I would stress to property masters the importance of seeing that properties that have been borrowed are returned, undamaged, as soon as possible after the close of a production, together with a brief note of thanks.

FIG 22   A specimen property plot – *Chu Chin Chow*

Act I Scene 5   Kasim Baba's Palace

3 Oriental carpets	DL, DR, C	O.T.
2 Carved stools (Double I.1)	ULC, URC	O.T.
Gong on stand with beater (Double I.1.)	Below L stool	O.T.
9 Oriental cushions	On carpets L and R	O.T.
2 Long bamboo poles	Gatekeepers	W.G.O.S.
Scroll (Double Desert Song)	Mukbill	E.H.S.
2 Incense censers	Boys	Rob
Incense	In censers	W.G.O.S.
24 assorted bags of money	Buyers and attendants	E.H.S. and Alan
Long staff (Double I.1.)	Abdullah	Fox
Rattle	Hasan's chinaman	Fox
Trick dagger	Zahrat	Fox
Special fan	Hasan	Vic T
18 Scimitars (Double I.3.)	Robbers	Fox

Act II Scene 1   Kasim Baba's Palace

Oriental carpet (Double I.5.)	UC	O.T.
Cushions (Double I.5.)	On carpet	O.T.
Small round table	R of cushions	O.T.
Hookah	DS of cushions	Trov.
Metal wine jar (Double I.1.)	On table	Rob
Plate of fruit (Double I.1.)	On table	Rob and E.H.S.
Gong with stand and beater (Double)	Above L cushion	O.T.
Dagger (Double I.5. Zahrat)	Solo dancer	Fox or Bapty
5 Bags of money (Double I.5.)	Ali's boys	E.H.S. and Alan
8 Javanese fans (Double I.1.)	Attendants	Fox

Act II Scene 2 In the starlight		
Nil		

Act II Scene 3 Cave		
6 Large jars (wire netting or cardboard in necks)	DL and UL	
Money, jewels, bottle tops	In tops of jars	W.G.O.S., E.H.S., Alan
8 Sacks (with wire netting)	L and R	Ted G
Money, jewels, bottle tops	In tops of sacks	W.G.O.S., E.H.S., Alan
Large trunk	DR	Rob
Money, jewels, bottle tops	In top of trunk	W.G.O.S., E.H.S., Alan
Post and chains	RC	S.S.
Goblets, silver trinket Boxes, candle sticks, }*ad lib* Fans, etc.	Various – see plan	W.G.O.S. and Rob
Gag and black gauze	Zahrat	Fox
18 Scimitars (Double I.3.)	Robbers	Fox

Act II Scene 4 Cherry Orchard		
Oriental carpet (Double I.5.)	DC	O.T.
Cushion (Double I.5.)	On carpet	O.T.
Plate of sweetmeats (Double I.1.)	On carpet	Rob and E.H.S.

Every production poses its own problems for the property master and it would be impossible to cover every eventuality he may have to contend with. However, there are certain items that constantly crop up in musicals which are worth considering here:

FIREARMS

These are constantly called for and range from duelling pistols and muzzle loaders to six-shooters and modern hardware. In many cases, they have to be practical. Specialist hire firms exist who can supply virtually every form of practical firearm suitable for stage use, but these can only be hired on production of a current firearms licence. It is a good plan for either the stage manager or property master to hold such a licence and to keep it up-to-date. Application should be made to any police station. Firearms should be kept under close supervision and locked away when not in use.

It is advisable to cover any shots that have to be made on the stage. Guns have a habit of misfiring in theatrical performances. In such an event, the actor should be instructed to retain his aim keeping his finger on the trigger, while the ever-watchful stage manager remedies matters with a shot from an automatic in the wings. If the stage manager is really on his toes, the audience will be unaware of the mishap.

In *Annie Get Your Gun*, repeater rifles play a big part and I have yet to be involved in a production where one or more have not jammed. The only way to avoid a bad stage gaffe is to prepare for such an emergency. Ensure that two additional loaded guns are on the stage during the shooting sequences, and in the event of a gun jamming, dialogue and business similar to the following is inserted:

ANNIE: 'Gun's jammed!'

BUFFALO BILL: 'Here, take another, Annie.' (*Hands her new gun, shooting continues*)

Early in the production, the producer can interrupt the shooting scenes with 'Gun jams!' so that all the actors concerned get used to switching to the amended dialogue, and if, unhappily, a gun does jam during the performances, most of the audience will accept it as part of the show.

FLOWERS

Flowers, either as posies, bridal bouquets, vast ornate stage decorations or merely single blooms feature in most musicals, and here a word of warning. There are now on the market many varieties of blooms fashioned from plastic material that look extremely natural, are cheap and are very hard wearing. Unfortunately, most makes are inflammable and do not respond to fireproofing, and if you use them you stand the risk of their being condemned by the fire inspector. Far better to fashion your own blooms from other material and treat them with one of the fireproofing liquids (see p. 86), or buy them from a reputable theatrical supplier. Although there is a superstition attached to the use of real flowers on the stage, the real reason is that natural blooms just will not stand up to the heat of the lanterns and wilt. There is also the danger of discarded foliage being left on the stage which may cause an actor or dancer to slip, and this no doubt gave rise to the superstition.

STAGE MEALS

Stage food is easy to concoct. When it has to be edible it should be something that is easy to cut and eat. Bananas, jelly and blancmange can be shaped and coloured to represent all manner of foods; they require little mastication and are easily swallowed. In any case, the amount of food that actually has to be eaten should be kept to the minimum, for actors cannot speak and sing with their mouths full. Large joints, chickens, pies, cakes and fruit can be fashioned from papier-mâché or moulded in latex.

It goes without saying that real alcoholic beverages are never used on the stage. Water, suitably coloured, will serve as most spirits and still wines, whilst ginger ale makes a convincing champagne. If a bottle has to be opened on the stage, by all means ensure that the cork moves freely, but do not forget to replace the foil cap so that the bottle does indeed appear to be fresh.

ANIMALS AND OTHER MATTERS

Animals are frequently involved in musicals and they come under the heading of properties (and go on the property list!). There are specialists who hire stage-trained animals and they will usually arrange their transport and control. Where possible the owner should be in charge of the animal on the stage, and given ample opportunity to rehearse it in the required moves. This should be done not only during the floor work, but under performance conditions with the full lighting and with the orchestra to accustom the animal to these.

Many smaller and specialized properties can be made by the property master, and here it is essential to indicate, in detail, exactly what you require. Sketches and working drawings should be produced before the work is put in hand, in order that the finished product complies with the director's requirements. The producer should have a basic knowledge of property making and there are many excellent publications on this aspect of stage-craft.

FIREPROOFING

As with scenery, all properties should be fireproofed, and the following solutions have been found suitable for this purpose:

Solution A   (for scenery and coarser fabrics)
             Boracic acid   15 oz
             Sodium phosphate   10 oz
             dissolved in 1 gallon of water
Solution B   Sal ammoniac   16 oz
             Borax   16 oz
             dissolved in 3 quarts of water
             This tends to be corrosive and a small amount of acetic acid can be added to counteract this.
Solution C   (for more delicate fabrics)
             Borax   10 oz
             Boracic acid   8 oz
             dissolved in 1 gallon of water

It should be borne in mind that if the material is washed, it will have to be treated afresh with a fireproofing solution. Fireproofing requirements vary from place to place and it is always advisable to confer with the local authority. However, as a guide, a simple test for flame-resistance is to hang a strip, at least one inch wide, of the fabric to be tested, in a draught-free place. Apply a naked flame to the centre of the bottom edge for five seconds. If less than one square inch has been consumed by flame at the end of one minute, the fireproofing may be regarded as satisfactory.

EFFECTS

Sound effects can be divided into two groups; those that are produced manually and those that are recorded on disc or tape. Chief among the manual variety are the sounds of wind, rain, various horns and hooters, hoofbeats and thunder, although even the first two are more often recorded.

A WIND MACHINE

This presents no difficulty for the amateur handyman. It is merely a slatted drum, mounted on an axle supported in a cradle and capable of being rotated by means of a handle. A length of silk or canvas is attached at one end to the cradle and passes over the drum. The other end is weighted and battened. When the drum is rotated a good wind sound is produced and the pitch can be varied by exerting pressure on the free end of the silk (see fig. 23).

THE SOUND OF RAIN

This can be effected with an apparatus very similar to a wind machine, but in this case the drum is slatted on the inside, and filled with a pint of dried peas. Turning the handle slowly produces the sound of gentle rain, if the speed is increased, that of a heavy downpour. An alternative is a long narrow box, fitted internally with cardboard baffles. Before closing the box, dried peas are added, the effect of the peas striking the baffles as they run from end to end of the box vividly reproduces the sound of rain (see fig. 24).

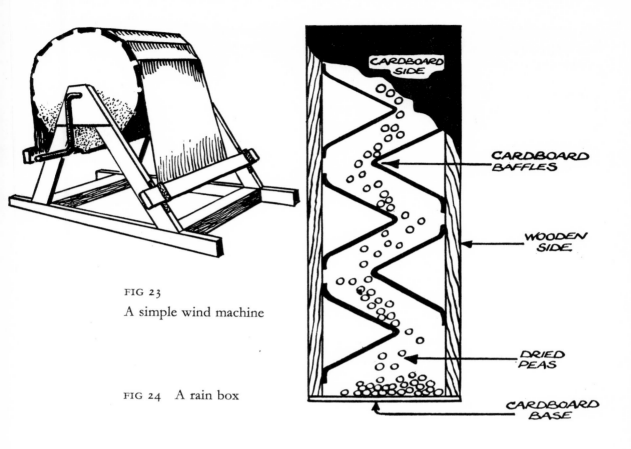

FIG 23
A simple wind machine

FIG 24 A rain box

RECORDINGS

But by far the majority of sound effects are obtained from recordings. Most recording companies have a large selection in their catalogues and several specialist firms exist who can supply all the effects for any given show. However, I do recommend the effects man to experiment with his own equipment, using both his own recordings as well as the commercial ones and above all, experimenting. I recall the fun a group of us had when we tried to simulate a motor launch pulling alongside a steamer. The final effect was achieved by using a montage of the following sounds:

Seagulls – commercial recording

Two-stroke motor-cycle ticking over – recorded live

Air being blown down a straw through a jug of water – recorded live

And all this was done in the front garden of a house on a summer Sunday morning! The sound effects cue sheet should give the duration of the effect, together with the sound level desired, as well as the 'standby' and 'go' cues (see specimen cue sheet, fig. 25).

VISUAL EFFECTS

These cover a field so vast and complex as to require a book solely devoted to the subject, and I can do no better than refer you to one of the many excellent publications listed in the bibliography. Many effects can be obtained with a special effects lantern – rain, clouds, fire and rainbows for example, but, as in the whole sphere of effects, it rests with the ingenuity and inventiveness of the effects man.

```
Finian's Rainbow effects cue sheet
No. 1                     After Overture to start Act 1
          TAPE            Harmonica music, sections 1 to 5 (Volume set at 8) (Tabs
                             open on cue)


No. 2   TAPE              Skylark trills
                          Cue: (p. 6 in lib.)
                             Finian: 'Why don't you try? It was the last . . .'
                          Fade in vol. 7 and hold until Sharon sings, then fade out
                             quickly


No. 3   TAPE              Night noises
                          Fade in over No. 4a in score – p. 24 (Bring up quickly to 8)
                          Continue until Finian places crock in hiding place, and
                             slowly fade


No. 4   MANUAL            Thunder clap and roll
                          Cue: (p. 27 in lib.)
                             Sharon: 'I wish to God he were
                          BLACK' – DBO   Lightning flash UR
                             Loud clap of thunder sf > p.
                          ACT 2


No. 5   TAPE              Car horn
                          End of 'Idle Rich' – p. 93 in score
                          Car horn heard UR, getting nearer (Start at vol 3, build to 8)
                          Continues to cue: 'Mr Hire and Mr Purchase'.
                                        Cut off


No. 6   MANUAL            Crack of thunder UL
                          Cue: (p. 47 in lib.)
                          Og: 'I wish you WHITE'. (LOUD crack) (Similar to cue 4)
                                        Finis
```

FIG 25   A specimen effects cue plot – *Finian's Rainbow*

THE PROMPTER

Of all the jobs connected with amateur musicals, I rate that of the prompter as being the most thankless. It is an extremely important task and far too often is given to someone at the last moment. Women usually make the best prompters, but whoever undertakes this position must be capable of sustained concentration. The prompter should attend rehearsals once the producer has roughed out the show so that she may be thoroughly conversant with the delivery of the speeches, the pace of the scene and where and when pauses are intended. Nothing is worse than to get a prompt in the middle of an artistic pause. She will also learn to recognize which of the various actors have a tendency to dry-up.

If a prompt proves necessary, it should be given clearly and loudly enough for the actor to pick it up. It does not matter if the audience hears it; the aim is to get the actor back on his lines. It is difficult to prompt in a musical item. Generally the musical director will supply the lines. In the case of concerted singing, one of the other principals may cover the individual's lapse of memory.

CALLS

Calls are given by the call boy. This title applies irrespective of the sex of the individual carrying out the duty. In a big musical being played in a large theatre it may prove advantageous to use more than one call boy. Their call sheets are made out by the stage manager and I prefer to let him tell the call boys when to make a call. It is also a good plan to have the call boy remind the principal actors of any personal properties they should bring to the stage. Many theatres have a public address system linking the stage manager to the various dressing rooms. This should, however, augment the services of the call boy rather than super-cede them.

STAGE HANDS

In addition to the people already mentioned, there will also be a number of stage hands. These will vary in number and be allocated various duties according to the size of the production, but their jobs will include those of curtain man, flyman, property men who carry the furniture, and what are called in America, grips. Grips handle the stage scenery, flats, ground rows and the like.

The stage manager should plot the tasks of each member of the stage crew during a scene change on a master work plot. Each individual is then given his own work sheet and scene changes are rehearsed under the direction of the stage manager. This ensures speedy and efficient changes and is frequently omitted by amateur companies. However pressed for time the company may be, the stage manager should insist on a scenery rehearsal.

Other departments which, strictly speaking, come under the heading of back-stage staff, are the wardrobe mistress and the make-up artist.

The Wardrobe Mistress should be in attendance backstage with her team of assistants, ready to cope with running repairs and minor alterations, and to see that any costumes that require pressing are dealt with.

MAKE-UP

It is the practice of most musical companies to engage a professional make-up artist. Nevertheless, it is highly desirable that all members should at least be capable of applying a competent straight make-up. It is physically impossible for a make-up man to cope with a full cast of fifty or more players, even with the help of one or two assistants. His talents are best saved for the make-up of the principals and for any character make-up that may be needed.

Since a musical is generally a large-scale production, requiring a large theatre, make-up for such a show tends to be somewhat heavier than that used for legitimate drama. How heavy it should be will depend on the size of the stage and auditorium and the intensity of the lighting. The producer and make-up artist should decide on the basic shades to be used, and be at pains to see that the cast achieve uniformity in their make-up.

The basic reasons for using make-up on the stage are three-fold:

1 To counteract the bleaching effect of stage lighting
2 To assist the actor to appear younger or older
3 To assist the actor to assume different national or racial characteristics

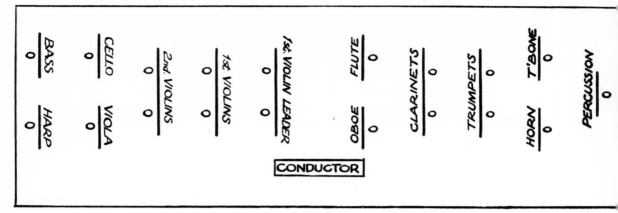

FIG 26   Layout for a pit orchestra

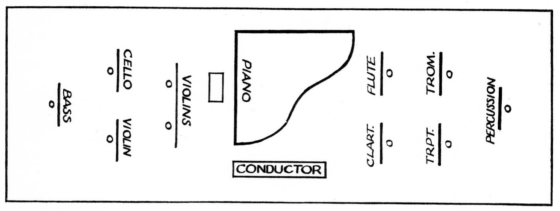

FIG 27   Layout for a small orchestra

There can be no hard and fast rules laid down for the application of make-up. Various types of unguents exist and a careful study of the different techniques will help, but only constant practice and experiment will bring expertise. Help is readily available from either of the two main theatrical cosmetic companies, Max Factor and Leichner, who will arrange lectures and demonstrations for the company, and the go-ahead society is urged to make full use of these facilities.

The make-up artist will require a room or secluded corner for his work, with sufficient space to lay out his equipment. The make-up chair should be strongly lit, to approximate the intensity of the stage lighting – a spare stage flood-light will serve this purpose. If the dressing rooms are not equipped with make-up tables, supplementary lighting and mirrors should be provided.

BAND ROOM

The stage manager should also try to arrange for a special room to be set aside for the orchestra, where they can retire when they are not required in the orchestra pit. Ideally this should be situated under the stage, with direct access to the orchestra pit. If space allows, a smaller room can be set aside for the sole use of the musical director. In addition, the stage manager should see that the orchestra pit is set out to the musical director's requirements, and that sufficient adequately illuminated music stands are available.

Musicals frequently involve quick costume changes for certain principals and, where no quick-change room is available, a corner of the stage which is not required for scenery can be screened off to afford a temporary dressing room.

A final point for the stage manager. If the production includes dances, he should arrange that resin boxes are provided at each side of the stage; the space behind the false proscenium is usually a suitable spot.

9 Lighting the show

'There's a bright golden haze on the meadow.'
OKLAHOMA!

INTRODUCTION

Why does one light a show? The reasons are I think two-fold. We need light in order that the audience may see the actors – their expressions, gestures, and movement. In many amateur musicals this would often appear to be as far as the producer wants to go, but good stage lighting must go well beyond this objective.

It should also create an environment, thus assisting the actors, through their interpretation of their parts, to bring to the audience the full meaning, character and mood of the playwright's script.

It is easy to light the players. It is also easy to light the set to give an interesting and plausible picture. The difficulty is to do both at the same time.

The professional producer with virtually unlimited time and resources at his command, usually has a lighting artist to design the plot in collaboration with him. The amateur producer, working under severe limitations has to rely on the local stage electrician, who, whilst an indispensible person when it comes to the wiring up and mounting of instruments, is usually an artisan and not an artist. That is not to say that many skilled technicians are not possessed of great artistic taste, but all too often the reverse is sadly true.

It therefore falls back on the producer to prepare his own lighting plot. This should have been prepared well before the first night, so that at the lighting call the producer knows what he wants to do and the means whereby he will achieve his ends.

VISIBILITY

We have already agreed that our prime purpose in lighting the stage is visibility – to enable our audience to see clearly those things which they should see. This does not mean that the stage should at all times be flooded with light. There may be certain things which they should either not see, or not see so distinctly.

PLAUSIBILITY

Whilst lighting for visibility we must also aim for feeling of plausibility on our stage. Decide upon the apparent source of light, for on this depends the whole lighting plot. In the main, scenes are illuminated either by natural light – the sun or the moon or artificial light – chandeliers, wall brackets, lanterns, fireplaces and so on, and we should attempt to simulate the light that one could reasonably expect to originate from these sources.

COMPOSITION

The lighting should enhance the stage picture, unifying the actors and their surroundings into a pleasing and meaningful composition. This may include adding emphasis to some highlights and shadows, the subduing of less important features and the general blending of light on those areas demanding equal illumination, thus unobtrusively focusing the audience's attention on those areas where the important action takes place.

MOOD

Finally there is the mood of the scene. This usually follows if the first three factors, visibility, plausibility and composition have been properly handled. It is possibly the most important aspect to consider but it must result from the amalgamation of the other factors.

INTENSITY

All light, no matter from what source, oil, gas or electricity, has certain qualities defined as intensity, colour, distribution and movement. The intensity of the light will vary from a mere glimmer to a burst of illumination of many hundreds of foot candles. The production may call for an intimate love scene played only in the light of a glowing fire, to be followed by an exterior scene in blazing sunlight. Between these extremes there are infinite variations available to the lighting designer. This flexibility is achieved by the use of resistances, or dimmers as they are called in the theatre.

COLOUR

The second quality of light is colour. Let me quote from Frederick Bentham of Strand Electric: 'That white light is the sensation of viewing several coloured lights simultaneously and that coloured light is something less than white light must be firmly fixed in the mind. A spotlight with a blue filter is a spotlight minus, not a spotlight plus.'

If you have ever seen a ray of sunlight passed through a prism you will know that refraction occurs and the spectrum appears – the white light has been split up into a band of coloured light ranging imperceptibly from violet, through blues, greens and yellows to red. Each of these colours has a different wave-length and if we cut out certain wave-lengths from a beam of white light we shall be left with a beam of coloured light. The simplest way to do this is by using colour filters. These are sheets of dyed plastic or gelatine which suppress the unwanted colours of the spectrum.

Strand Electric issue sample swatches and their range and colours have now been adopted by most principal firms as the British standard for the stage. The range is as follows:

1	Yellow	5a	Deep orange	10	Middle rose
2	Light amber	6	Primary red	11	Dark pink
3	Straw	7	Light rose	12	Deep rose
4	Medium amber	8	Deep salmon	13	Magenta
5	Orange	9	Light salmon	14	Ruby

15 Peacock blue	32 Medium blue	49 Canary
16 Blue-green	33 Deep amber	50 Pale yellow
17 Steel blue	34 Golden amber	51 Gold tint
18 Light blue	35 Deep golden amber	52 Pale gold
19 Dark blue	36 Pale lavender	53 Pale salmon
20 Deep blue (primary)	(surprise pink)	54 Pale rose
21 Pea green	38 Pale green	55 Chocolate tint
22 Moss green	39 Primary green	56 Pale chocolate
23 Light green	40 Pale blue	57 Pink
24 Dark green	41 Bright blue	60 Pale grey
25 Purple	42 Pale violet	61 Slate blue
26 Mauve	43 Pale navy blue	62 Turquoise
27 Smoky pink	45 Daylight	63 Sky blue
29 Heavy frost	46 Chrome yellow	66 Pale red
30 Clear	47 Apricot	67 Steel tint
31 Light frost	48 Bright rose	

The whole question of colour mixing is an extremely complex one which merits investigation by the producer who would fully understand the resources at his command. Certainly every producer should be on the Strand Electric mailing list for their excellent free magazine *Tabs*, and a visit to this company's demonstration theatre to witness the illustrated lectures on all aspects of stage lighting will pay dividends.

DISTRIBUTION

The third quality of light is distribution. This varies not only according to the source, but also from hour to hour, season to season and clime to clime.

For example, compare the harsh brilliance of sunlight at high noon at the equator with the gentle wash of light on a grey, hazy English autumn day. Or again consider the variations obtainable from different domestic light fittings; compare the pendant fixture, a reading lamp and a fluorescent tube.

There is a large variety of stage lanterns to assist the producer to simulate these various effects. Each lantern has been designed for a specific purpose and will distribute its light in a certain way, and the producer should acquaint himself with the differing properties of the lanterns at his command.

MOVEMENT

The last quality of light is movement. Natural light is forever changing. Take as an example an interior on a summer's afternoon. Bright sunlight streams through the windows. Time passes and the daylight gradually fades (movement in intensity), and the beams of light sink lower as the sun sets (movement of distribution), and get cooler (movement in colour). Finally the sun sinks and the general tones of dusk illuminate the room (movement of distribution).

EQUIPMENT AND ITS FUNCTION

Let us now take a brief look at the more usual equipment at our disposal with which we shall attempt to plan our lighting plot.

By far the most important and the most useful group are the spotlights. These can be divided into two main groups – the profile spots and the Fresnels. As their name implies, the profile spotlights have a hard edge. They come in all sizes from the small, but very useful and efficient 250 watt, to the great sunspot arcs. The Fresnels come in the same sizes but, the Fresnel lens softens the edge of the spot and the light blends with the surrounding lighting whilst giving emphasis to the place on which it is focused.

Pageant lanterns which are spotlights giving parallel beams of light, and which were often used to simulate rays of the sun, are now largely discontinued, having been replaced by 1,000 and 2,000-watt Fresnel spots or Beam lights.

Acting area and arena floods which come in 1,000 and 2,000-watt sizes are de-signed to hang vertically down on the stage. These are extremely useful for giving washes of light to given areas.

Battens and footlights are perhaps the only fixtures you can be certain of finding in any community theatre and, unfortunately, they are probably the least useful. They are generally six-foot lengths divided into compartments and wired for three circuits. Apart from the back batten which will certainly be required for lighting the backcloth or the cyclorama, I usually disconnect the footlights and other battens and use the circuits and dimmers saved for other lanterns.

The musical show is a big colourful type of entertainment and the follow spot is nearly always essential. These lanterns which used to be called limes, or arcs, are nowadays incandescent lamps of intense brilliance. Utilizing an iris, these spots can be narrowed down to a pin spot or opened up and 'boxed' to take in a front stage line-up. They are generally housed in a special projection room at the back of the gallery and are manually operated.

POSITIONING THE SPOTLIGHTS

Mr Bentham maintains that the apparatus used to light the actor should be kept separate from that used to light the settings. This is rarely possible for amateurs and some compromise is inevitable. Where should the lanterns be placed in order to reveal the actor's features and at the same time give some degree of natural modelling to his face? Artists tend to sketch their subjects as though the source of light falls from above at an angle of 45°. This principle is generally adopted by most stage lighting designers by lighting the actor, and the instrument most favoured is the spotlight – the 45° angle being sought in both the vertical and horizontal planes.

An actor's face which has been lit in this manner with a single spotlight, takes on great character – his features and expression being clearly visible, but from one side only. Therefore, another similarly angled instrument is needed to illuminate the other side of the face, although this tends to wash out the effect of the first. To counteract such lack of plasticity colour can be used; a warm tint on one side, a cool tint on the other. We can find the reasoning for this if we observe nature. Direct sunlight hits the subject on one side with all its warmth and intensity: the other side of the subject receives reflected light from the surroundings and this light will be cooler and less strong in intensity.

The colours for these spotlights is a matter of personal preference and will depend on the overall lighting and scenic conception of the production, but generally I find that 51 Gold tint or 52 Pale gold is most suitable for the warm side, with 54 Pale rose on the cool side as a satisfactory mix.

Sufficient of these spotlights are needed to ensure that all the acting areas of the stage receive an equal spread of light. Actors must not be subject to distracting surges of light as they move about. For the average size stage used by musical companies, six pairs of lanterns will usually suffice, the stage being divided into six areas for this purpose. The conventional method is to number these areas from one to six reading from DL to UR (see fig. 18 on page 66). Supplementary lighting – spots and lanterns ranged along the sides of the stage – is often added to give cross light. This should be set fairly high since an actor playing near the side of the stage may find himself in distractingly bright light.

Top lighting or back lighting is another variation when the instruments are mounted overhead to shine down or slightly forward of the actors, thereby creating a halo effect about the head and upper body and making the actors stand out from their background.

STRIPLIGHTS

Battens and footlights, once so popular, are not regarded with the same importance as they once were. Such forms of lighting trace their ancestry back to the earliest days of oil (hence floats) and gas. They have tended to become hallowed by tradition and yet of all equipment they are probably the least essential. They are useful adjuncts to the lanterns already discussed and serve to blend the light and iron out any unevenness created by the spotlights. They should be used with discretion, particularly the footlights which have an unfortunate habit of creating shadows on the backcloth.

LIGHTING THE BACKGROUNDS

Having lit the actors we now turn to their backgrounds. In most musicals these consist of a backcloth or a cyclorama and need rows of very powerful instruments both above and below to give a wash of light of sufficient intensity to blend over the whole surface.

The top of the cyclorama is usually lit by the upstage batten using three circuits. Often this is supplemented with floods.

Before colouring up three circuits make certain that you will be using them all. Often the cyclorama can be lit with one circuit blues and the other two ways left open or frosted.

If you are lucky enough to get your backcloth skies painted in aniline dye (with the landscape painted in the usual opaque scenic colours) you will be able to back-light the sky. This gives a wonderfully transluscent effect. The battens should be flown very high up behind the cloth and point almost directly down it. A strip of plain white canvas hung upstage of the batten will reflect any stray light and give additional punch.

Bottom lighting comes from the ground rows. These can be magazine ground rows or footlight lengths. In either case they will need to be masked, either with scenery or behind rostra. Failing this a long narrow plywood flat propped against the downstage edge of the batten at an angle of 35° or less to the stage will mask the lanterns. Painted a matt white it will pick up any top lighting and blend with the cyclorama. Ideally, ground rows should be at least twenty-four inches from the backcloth or cyclorama in order that the colours of the ground row may blend; if they are closer than this, spottiness will occur.

SPECIAL EFFECTS

In addition to all this equipment, use can be made of special-effects lanterns. These often find a place in the lighting set-up of a musical, and used with taste and discretion can be very telling. Time and patience is required to locate the optimum position for the best results. When ordering effects lanterns it is advisable to tell the supplier the length of throw you require together with the desired size of the projected effect, in order that they may send you the appropriate lens. Static effects, such as the rainbow in *Finian's Rainbow* require only one circuit (on a dimmer), whilst moving effects – clouds, rain, water – require an additional circuit for the electric motor. The lamp can be wired through a dimmer so that dissolves and fades can be achieved, but the motor tends to stick if 'faded in'.

To control all this equipment it is often necessary to bring in subsidiary switch-boards. Various patterns are available for hire: eight- and twelve-way slider dimmer-boards to take 300-, 500- or 1,000-watt loads, as well as six-, eight- or twelve-way interlocking dimmerboards to carry from 500- to 2,000-watt loads on each circuit. As the name implies, the latter can be interlocked into banks of fourteen, twenty or twenty-four ways or more if required, but multiple dimmerboards of this size are bulky and require several operators. However, we can look forward to the compact and versatile Thysiter dimmers being available for hire in the near future.

THE LIGHTING PLOT

When planning a lighting plot, the first thing that is required is a scale drawing of the stage, showing all the various settings. These can be indicated in various coloured inks or by varied broken lines. Next mark all the permanently fixed lighting equipment. Until recently there has been no standardized set of symbols with which to indicate the positions of the various types of lanterns. However, at a meeting of an expert committee of the Commission International d'Eclairage held in Prague in 1966, general agreement was reached over the acceptance of certain basic symbols for lanterns. These are due to be ratified at the full CIE Conference in Washington in 1967 and once this is done, it is to be hoped that they will be universally accepted and understood. The proposed symbols, with definitions are shown in fig. 28. Once the position of the additional equipment has been decided and plotted it is numbered in the following order. Starting at the bottom right of the diagram or, if you prefer, downstage prompt side, the spots are numbered from right to left. Continue numbering the floods, footlights and battens, then the specials: smoke boxes, chandeliers, wall sconces. This done, a start can be made on the details of the set-up. These are:

a) The number of the equipment
b) The type of lantern
c) Where it is hung
d) What is its purpose
e) What wattage lamp
f) What colour medium (if any)
g) Any special remarks

A specimen set-up sheet will be found on page 99. A copy of this together with the scale drawing should be sent to the resident electrician, who should know exactly the equipment required and what he will need to hire. Furthermore, he will be able to start hanging some of the equipment in advance, thus saving valuable time at the dress rehearsal.

An example For the purpose of illustrating the designing of a lighting plot I am quoting from my own set-up for *The Wizard of Oz* which was played at Hornsey Town Hall in 1966. *The Wizard of Oz* is an extremely complex show. It is written in two acts, with one interval and the synopsis of scenes reads as follows:

Act I
  i A Kansas Farm
     First Interlude
  ii Munchkinland
     Second Interlude
  iii On the road to Munchkinland
     Third Interlude
  iv The Yellow Brick Road
     Interval

Act II
  v Emerald City
  vi The Witches' Castle
    a) The Parlour
    b) The Great Hall
     Fourth Interlude
  vii Emerald City

For production purposes we condensed scene 6 into one set, playing in black trailers as background for the skeleton dance which was lit by ultra violet light.

The interludes were placed before gold trailers, a festoon drop curtain and landscape tabs. Since no sets of costumes were in existence and the only scenery available required a grid, which we did not have, it was decided to design the production from scratch.

Apart from scene 1 which was played naturalistically, the rest of the show was pure fantasy, the designs being based on a child's picture book.

Hornsey stage presents many of the snags and difficulties which the amateur producer will come across when he has not the advantages of a professional theatre. The stage has a permanent proscenium arch measuring 40 feet by 18 feet high and 18 feet from the back wall of the stage. For musical productions a false proscenium made of velvet complete with house tabs is hung 8 feet in front of this to give an opening of 38 feet 6 inches by 18 feet high. There is no apron to the stage and no lanterns can be slung in the 8-feet gap between the permanent proscenium and the false proscenium.

An extension was constructed either side of the false proscenium measuring 6 feet deep by 18 feet wide giving the effect of an apron either side of the orchestra pit. This served two purposes.

It gave us somewhere to place our lighting towers for our FOH boom lights

FIG 28   Proposed symbols for lanterns

1 Floodlight
2 Special floodlight
3 Reflector spotlights
4 Sealed beam lamp
5 Lens spotlight

6 Fresnel spotlight
7 Profile spotlight
8 Effects spotlight
9 Softlight/battens
10 Bifocal spotlight
   (introduced by Strand Electric)

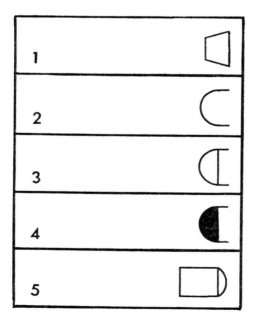

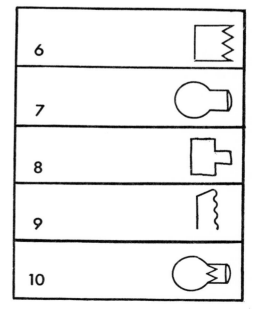

FIG 29   Specimen lighting set up for *Wizard of Oz* (see also figs. 30, 31)

FIG 30

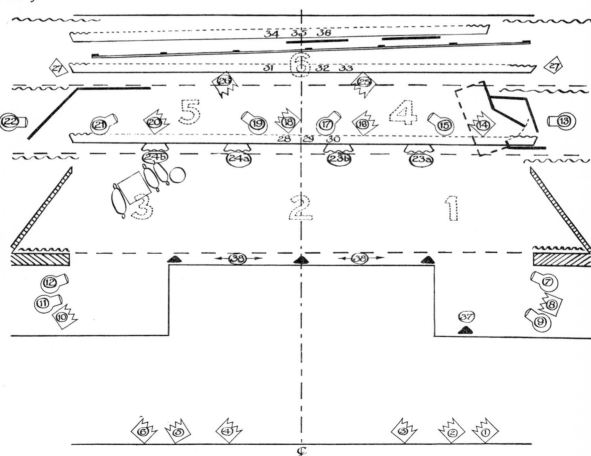

No.	Instrument	Location	Purpose	Lamp	Colour	Remarks
1.	8" Fresnel Spot	F.O.H Bar	Area 2L Warm	1000W	51	
2.	" " "	" "	" 3L Warm	"	51	
3.	" " "	" "	" 1L Warm	"	51	Barn Doors
4.	" " "	" "	" 1R Cool	"	45	" "
5.	" " "	" "	" 3R Cool	"	45	" "
6.	" " "	" "	" 2R Cool	"	45	
7.	Profile Spot	Boom L	" 2,3	500W	Green	Cauldron
8	8" Fresnel Spot	" "	" 2,3	1000W	52	
9.	Profile Spot	" "	" 5	500W	51	
10	8" Fresnel Spot	Boom R.	" 2,1.	1000W	45	
11	Profile Spot	" "	" 2,	500W	Green	T/V Set
12	" "	" "	" 4	500W	45	
13	" "	Stand U.L	Crosslight	500W	52	
14	6" Fresnel Spot	Batt 1. Pipe	Area 4L Warm	500W	52	} Paired
15	Profile Spot	" "	" 4L Cool	500W	45	
16	6" Fresnel Spot	" "	" 4R Warm	500W	52	} Paired
17.	Profile Spot	" "	" 4R Cool	500W	45	
18	6" Fresnel Spot	" "	" 5L Warm	500W	52	} Paired
19	Profile Spot	" "	" 5L Cool	500W	45	
20	6" Fresnel Spot	" "	" 5R Warm	500W	52	} Paired
21	Profile Spot	" "	" 5R Cool	500W	45	
22	Profile Spot	Stand U.R	Crosslight	500W	45	
23	Acting Areas	Down of	Downlight	1000W	2	} Paired
3/b	" "	Batt 1.	"	1000W	2	
24	Acting Areas	" "	"	1000W	2	} Paired
3/b	" "	"	"	1000W	2	
25	8" Fresnel Spot	Batt 2 Pipe	Backlight	1000W	51	
26	" " "	" "	"	1000W	51	
27	} Floodlight	Stand U.L	Backings	1000W	2/16/22	} Paired
27		" U.R	"	1000W	2/16/22	
28	} Batten	—	—	—	45	3 Circuits
29	No 1.	—	—	—	45	Independant
30		—	—		Open	
31	} Batten	—	—	—	45	3 Circuits
32	No 2	—	—	—	Open	Independant
33		—	—	—	16	
34		—	—	—	45	3 Circuits
35	Ground Row	—	—	—	Open	Independant
36		—	—	—	22	
37	Flash/Smoke Box			Used	Witch's Entrance	
38	U/V Floods (3)			Use	No Dimmers	

FIG 31

and also encircled the orchestra into a closer semblance of an orchestra pit. The lighting towers were constructed by our own staff and masked with black flats.

The house equipment consisted of footlights, two battens, and dips, all wired for three ways and controlled by twelve dimmers, each colour-way capable of being interlocked but no master interlocking device.

The dips were usually used to supply the four acting area lanterns. In addition, there were twelve 500-watt profile spots on the FOH bar; these were paired and controlled by six slider dimmers!

Lightingwise, this meant that the set-up had to cover both natural exteriors and a large number of varied sets using unnatural fantastic lighting.

Following the lines already discussed, a preliminary set-up was drawn out and sent to the stage manager and the resident electrician. It came back with the remark that we would overload the board and existing output from the main supply. So we had to compromise. The lanterns and sources of illumination that were absolutely essential were retained. Of the rest, some were deleted, others were changed to a similar lantern of lower wattage, and in other cases, pairs of lanterns were coupled into one circuit.

Figs. 29, 30, 31 indicate the set-up for this show. Areas 1, 2 and 3 were bounded upstage by the no 1 gold trailers, the no 2 festoon tabs and the no 3 landscape tabs, all of which were hung very closely together.

Areas 4 and 5 extended from the no 1 gold trailer line upstage, to be bounded by the line of the no 4 black trailers. Beyond this line lay area 6 extending upstage to the cyclorama.

To provide the punch of light required in the downstage areas 1, 2 and 3, six 1,000-watt profile spots were slung from the FOH bar. Two 1,000-watt Fresnel spots were also used to cover the centre and all these lanterns were focused well downstage. This is common practice in most musicals where the actors often come right down to the very edge of the apron, and they must be lit as brightly there as when they are confined by the 'fourth wall'.

To light areas 4 and 5 four Fresnel and four profile spots (500 watts) were used.

In the absence of booms, lanterns for downstage side-lighting were hung in our special tormentor towers. Two 1,000-watt Fresnel spots covered area 2; 500-watt profile spots were used for the Witches' scene, and two further 500-watt profiles were used to add punch to areas 4 and 5.

For down-light, use was made of the existing acting area lanterns, whilst back-lighting came from two 1,000-watt Fresnel spots mounted on no 1 batten. To blend the upstage lighting, batten one was used.

The cyclorama lighting came from batten two and ground rows, each using three independent circuits. The footlights were disconnected and the circuits saved were used for other lanterns.

A special feature of this show is the skeleton dance and to light the luminous-painted costumes, three ultra violet floods were installed in the floats. This necessitated using blue lamps in the orchestra stands, since the usual bulbs would have adversely affected the ultra violet effect.

Special fittings include flash and smoke boxes which were placed in convenient positions about the stage as and when they were required. The Wizard himself, a massive 12-foot high figure, had his own interior illumination and amplification; a rainbow, wing floods, microphones, tape desk for effects and follow spots all needed a source of supply. Nevertheless, the number of lanterns, equipment and dimmers used for this production was a very modest one, as indeed it had to be on a limited budget.

10 *Opening night and after*

> *'There's no business like Show Business!'*
> ANNIE GET YOUR GUN

Publicity and the front of house

The producer's work will be greatly enhanced if the front of the house is made as attractive and welcoming as possible. Everything should be done to give the audience the feeling that 'this is an occasion'. Admittedly this is not the producer's province, but the wise one will take an interest in front-of-house arrangements and will often diplomatically suggest methods of improvement; for let us admit, some amateur societies sadly neglect this aspect of the production.

Obviously the show must be well publicized. Striking posters boldly displayed at the entrance to the building should be well illuminated. It is often worth installing special lighting in order to offer your audience a cheerful approach to the theatre. The foyer should be bright and gay with photographs of the leading artists, past shows and scenes from the current production. In addition, tasteful floral arrangements can help to set the scene. In short, what is really required for a successful front-of-house atmosphere is a sense of showmanship.

Seating arrangements and cloakrooms should be clearly signposted and a notice indicating the time that the performance ends will all assist your audience.

The front-of-house staff are under the control of the front-of-house manager. William Lowry, doyen of house managers, having worked over sixty shows: *'If both the manager and his assistants can wear evening dress the feeling of the occasion is further heightened. The manager should ensure that all parts of the theatre have sufficient stewards to usher the public to their seats as well as an adequate number of programme-sellers. Arrangements should be made for the latter to be provided with a float of small change and all the front-of-house staff should be equipped with small pocket torches to assist in dealing with latecomers.'* The front-of-house manager should be advised of any dignitaries who are expected to attend and it is his responsibility to greet them and make them welcome. Often he will be assisted in this by officers of the company who are not otherwise engaged in the production. Wherever possible a private retiring room should be set aside for the entertaining and refreshment of the press and special guests in the intervals.

Warning that the curtain is about to rise can be given either by bells situated in the foyer and the bars or by an amplified announcement relayed from the stage to these parts of the theatre. It is normal to indicate that the curtain will rise in five minutes, three minutes and one minute. I make it a practice that once the house lights are lowered, the doors are closed and late-comers barred from taking their seats until the conductor has entered the pit and begun the overture. Only then are late-comers shown quietly to their seats. By using this method and making a habit of starting my shows punctually I now have very little trouble with late arrivals.

BACKSTAGE PROCEDURE

Let us now retire backstage and consider the procedure at a performance. The cast will have been instructed to be at the theatre at least a half an hour before the performance is timed to begin. This will allow them time to get changed and made up in a leisurely manner and avoids any last minute panic. Each actor should sign in on arrival and for this purpose lists are displayed on the dressing-room doors. This affords an easy check to the call-boy when giving the first call half an hour before the performance begins. Subsequent calls are made at quarter of an hour and five minutes before the rise of the curtain; the final call being 'overture and beginners, please'.

The orchestra should have a dressing room set aside for them and should not enter the orchestra pit until instructed to do so by the stage manager, through the call-boy. Just before they are despatched to their places the floats can be brought up on the house tabs. This is an added reminder to the audience that the show is about to begin and heightens the air of expectancy.

Then the stage manager cues the house lights and sends the conductor to the pit. Where possible he should be 'spotted' when he takes his place. Whether the spot is held on him during the overture is a matter for personal preference, but care should be taken to see that no light spills into the eyes of the musicians adjacent to the conductor.

THE NATIONAL ANTHEM

Should the National Anthem be played, and, if so, at the beginning or the end of the performance? Again this is a matter of choice, but I find the following practice convenient. If the show has an overture, 'The Queen' is played at the end and is sung by the full company. If there is no overture, the anthem is played at the beginning, or omitted, save at the last performance, when it is played at the end.

It is worth mentioning here that, if the National Anthem is to be sung by the company, it should be rehearsed as thoroughly as any of the other vocal items. Too often one hears versions using *ad lib*. harmonies and a variety of arrangements. It must be considered as part of the total performance and rehearsed as such.

THE STAGE MANAGER'S ROLE DURING THE PERFORMANCE

The performances are entirely in the hands of, and under the direction of, the stage manager. Alan Legget who has stage-managed many amateur musical shows for a number of companies, as well as having assisted backstage in several professional productions makes these observations:

'For a successful show there must be good backstage discipline from the whole company at all times. This will include observing the 'NO SMOKING' regulations, keeping entrances and exits clear, coming to the stage only when called and keeping quiet in the wings – in

general conducting oneself in an orderly and sensible way. The stage crew too, must be on their toes throughout the run and any slackness on their part must not be tolerated. All round co-operation is the hall-mark of success. Take a pride in the tidyness of your stage. See that the house tabs are well hung, and in good condition. Keep any cables that have to be visible to the minimum and neatly laid out. Any front-of-house lanterns should be positioned so as not to distract from the stage itself – watch for any stray light escaping into the eyes of the audience. Never, never allow the company to pass through the house curtain to gain access to the theatre and strictly prohibit any "peeping through the curtain". Visitors should not be allowed backstage until the end of the performance and then only by permission of the stage manager. Nor should the actors be allowed to leave the backstage area in costume or make-up – a common failing with amateurs.

'One of the many problems confronting a stage manager is the question of local fire safety regulations. Early in the week of the show, or during the dress rehearsal the local fire officer or his deputy will visit the theatre to check that all local fire regulations are being observed. His co-operation and goodwill should be diplomatically fostered since he has the power to close a theatre if he is dissatisfied with the existing fire precautions. Unfortunately, many of these fire officers have little practical knowledge of conditions backstage and they need to be carefully and quietly educated. Make certain that your staff play their part by seeing that adequate fire-fighting equipment is provided, maintained and is easily accessible. Be certain that the dressing rooms contain extinguishers and blankets and that no unauthorized electrical apparatus, such as electric fires or irons, is used in them.

'The stage manager's job does not finish with the fall of the final curtain. He and his staff must attend to the despatch of the scenery, costumes, furniture, properties and electrical equipment, ensuring that everything is returned to its rightful owner. The stage must be restored to its original condition; borders, legs and tabs that were removed for the production must be re-hung and everything left in a neat and tidy state. It pays to take trouble over this final task and your actions will endear you to both the theatre management and the hiring contractors and ensure that any future business you do with them receives the fullest co-operation.'

There is, naturally, a state of nervous tension on opening night. This is the time when the producer should exude encouragement; no matter what his personal feelings are regarding the production, he must devote his energies before the performance to quietly instilling confidence into his players. An occasional reminder, quietly given, may not be amiss, but this is no time for last-minute changes of plan. Just before the actors are called to the stage, a quick round of the dressing rooms to give a cheery 'Good Luck!' and then *he should quit the backstage area until the performance is over,* leaving the running of the show entirely to the stage manager.

THE PRODUCER AND THE PERFORMANCE

Perhaps the hardest job for the producer is watching the actual performance. He will see every little mistake: the exit that is not timed nearly as well as it was at dress rehearsal; the slight fluffing over lines – all these are magnified a hundred-fold because he knows what should have happened. Take heart – the audience rarely see these 'disastrous incidents' which, after all, happen to even the finest professional companies. By all means take notes and have a general call at the end of the evening, but use the occasion to praise and encourage as far as possible, tempering any criticism with humour and understanding.

Later in the run it may be necessary to check any tendency to slackness, both in delivery and reaction on stage and discipline off stage, but if the company take a pride in their work they will rarely need reminding of this.

The final performances do need watching, and one must guard against a party atmosphere overtaking the performance. A reminder to the company that the last night audience have come to see, and indeed have a right to see, a polished performance and that the celebrations do not start until after the curtain is down, will generally do the trick.

A word here about bouquets and other tributes that are sent to the cast. Very often the final show is prolonged indefinitely whilst these are handed over the footlights to all and sundry, to be followed by speeches and votes of thanks. If this grows out of hand it results in an impatient and rapidly diminishing audience and a restless and embarrassed cast.

If floral tributes are given publicly, let them be kept to the minimum and *rehearse* the procedure. The simplest method is to limit the bouquets to the principal ladies, all other offerings being sent to the dressing rooms or presented privately after the performance. Depending on the production of the *finale ultimo*, the flowers can either be handed over the footlights, when the lady's escort can receive and pass them to her, or the individuals can collect them in the wings and make their final entrance with them.

Usually the choreographer, musical director and producer will be introduced by a member of the cast or the committee and he should be advised as to where they will make an entrance. It is also advisable to limit the time allowed for the curtain speech – two minutes is more than enough – after which the musical director can lead the company in the National Anthem and the curtain is lowered for the last time.

CRITICS AND CRITICISM
During the performances the producer will have had an opportunity to assess the results of his labours. For perhaps the first time since rehearsals commenced he will be able to take a rather more detached view of the production and inevitably he will see its shortcomings.

Unfortunately, he will rarely receive reliable informed criticism. Audiences at amateur performances are invariably indulgent and will receive both an outstanding and a mediocre production with equal enthusiasm, while, all too often, the local critic will write his column with an eye to the circulation figures. Consequently neither the producer nor the actors get a proper assessment of their efforts.

This is regrettable since an honest and fair critical analysis of the production, accepted in the right spirit, can only serve to improve the all-round standard of both the producer's and actors' work. Some local critics, as well as the London section of Noda are working to this end and their constructive remarks are proving most valuable.

Sometimes the local critic can be persuaded to give his unbiased opinion to the company privately, but it should be the producer himself who is in the best position to honestly assess the show. Even if he cannot make his comments known to the company (there is always the next engagement to consider) he should be prepared to weigh up his endeavours and evaluate them for future reference. Any short-comings should be noted so that no repetition occurs in future productions. If he has prepared the show thoroughly, these should be relatively few, but I have yet to witness one of my own productions with which I was entirely satisfied. Let the last word go to my dear friend and musical director, Sydney Lockerman who had a habit of saying: 'The best production I have ever done, is the one I am working on at the moment!'

Finale ultimo

'Keep out of trouble with the law.'
PINK CHAMPAGNE

The producer is rarely required to deal with legal matters pertaining to the amateur theatre. These should be dealt with by the secretary and business manager for the company. However, since it is desirable to 'keep out of trouble with the law' as Dr Blind remarks in *Pink Champagne*, a few general pointers may be of assistance.

COPYRIGHT

As will be seen in the list of musical shows available for amateur presentation, most are still in copyright and permission must be sought from the copyright owner to present the work. Failure to do so would render the society liable to prosecution for such an offence and may incur them in heavy damages.

It should be noted that it covers the music, libretto and the lyrics and subsists during the lifetime of the author or composer and for fifty years after death. Since a musical show is usually the work of two or more persons (composer and librettist for example), the complete work will not be out of copyright until fifty years after the death of the last survivor of the authorship.

Once a show is out of copyright, as in the case of Gilbert and Sullivan operas, you are free to perform it without permission from any one or payment of performing fees.

There are many new versions or adaptations of old shows, the original of which may be out of copyright, but these new versions constitute a new work and royalties will probably be payable.

The Law of Copyright is an involved and complex one. There is, however, a very concise and explicit chapter on this and other legal aspects in Roy Stacey's *Running an Amateur Society*, which is published in the *Practical Stage Handbooks* series by Herbert Jenkins.

STAGE PLAY LICENCE

If you should be asked to produce an original work which has never been performed in public, you will have to ensure that it has been granted a stage play licence by the Lord Chamberlain's Office. This licence is issued only to the manager of the theatre and the play cannot be licensed until a production for a specified date has been arranged.

A typed manuscript of the play must be submitted to the Comptroller, Lord Chamberlain's Office, St James's Palace, London, SW1 at least seven days prior to the first performance. It should be accompanied by the date and place of first production and the reading fee. The latter is two guineas and should be made payable to the Examiner of Plays. Only the libretto and lyrics need to be submitted and these are kept by the Lord Chamberlain's Office for record purposes.

THEATRE LICENCES

Most societies present their shows in a theatre or hall which is licensed for theatrical performances, and there is seldom any worry over this section of the *Theatres Act* 1843. The relevant passage reads:

'It shall not be lawful for any person to have or keep any house or other place of public resort in Great Britain for the public performance of stage plays, without a licence: and every person who shall offend against this enactment shall be liable to forfeit such a sum as shall be awarded by the Court, not exceeding Twenty Pounds of every day on which such house or place shall have been so kept open by him for the purpose aforesaid without legal authority.'

SUNDAY PERFORMANCES

Whilst musical entertainments are permitted under the *Sunday Entertainments Act* 1932 at any place licensed for that purpose on a Sunday, the performances of stage plays (and a musical constitutes a stage play) are not permitted. Even if permission is obtained from the local authority for a public performance in aid of charity, it will only be granted on the understanding that no make-up or costume be worn and no patter or cross-talk is used.

UNIFORMS ON THE STAGE

It is illegal to wear an exact replica of any military, naval, air force or police uniform in a stage presentation (c.f. the *Uniforms Act* 1894 and the *Police Act* 1919). This injunction is overcome by making slight deviations to the actual uniform in the question of buttons, badges and so forth.

CHILDREN ON THE STAGE

So many modern musicals require child performers and the act with which one most frequently comes into conflict is *Section 22* of the *Children and Young Persons Act* 1933:

'1   *Subject to the provisions of this section a child shall not, except under and in accordance with the provisions of a licence granted and in force thereunder, take part in any entertainment in connection with which any charge, whether for admission or not, is made to any of the audience; and every person who causes or procures a child, or being his parent or guardian allows him, to take part in an entertainment in contravention of this section, shall, on summary conviction, be liable to a fine not exceeding five pounds, or, in the case of a second or subsequent offence, not exceeding twenty pounds.*

'2   *Subject as hereinafter provided and without prejudice to the provisions of this Part of this Act and any byelaws made thereunder with respect to employment, a licence under this section shall not be necessary for a child to take part in an entertainment if:*

(a) he has not during the preceding six months taken part on more than six occasions in entertainments in connection with which any such charge as aforesaid was made: and

(b) the net proceeds of the entertainment are devoted to purposes other than the private profit of the promoters. Provided that this subsection shall not apply in the case of an entertainment given in premises which are licensed for the sale of any intoxicating liquor unless either:

(i) these premises are also licensed for the public performance of stage plays or for public music, singing or dancing; or

(ii) special authority for the child to take part in the entertainment has been granted in writing under the hands of two justices of the peace.

'3   *Subject to such restrictions and conditions as may be prescribed by rules made by the Board of Education, a local authority may grant a licence for a child who has attained the age of twelve years and is residing in their area to take part in any specified entertainment or series of entertainments, whether within or without that area.'*

This is taken to mean that a child under school-leaving age may take part in up to six performances in any six months without licence. Children over twelve may take part in more than six performances, but only under licence, while children under twelve may, under no circumstances, take part in more than six performances.

Licences are granted by the local authority and they will require birth and medical certificates, photographs and a report from the child's teacher or headmaster.

There are several other legal aspects which the secretary should be acquainted with and reference should be made to:

Manual of Safety Requirements in Theatres and Other Places of Public Entertainment issued by the Home Office; *The Fire-Arms Act*, 1937, Section 4 (10).

Notices nos 9, 89 *and* 96 obtainable from HM Customs and Excise Authorities in addition to those already referred to.

Appendix

THE WOOD GREEN OPERATIC SOCIETY RULES

1 The Society shall be called THE WOOD GREEN OPERATIC SOCIETY.
2 The objects of the Society shall be the cultivation of the Arts of Music and Drama, particularly among the young of the district, and the encouragement of public appreciation of those Arts.
3 The funds of the Society shall be applied solely to the stated objects of the Society, and to Charitable and Philanthropic purposes.
4 No member of the Society shall receive payment directly or indirectly for services to the Society or for other than legitimate expenses incurred in its work.
5 In the event of the dissolution of the Society the remaining funds shall be devoted to objects similar to those of the Society or to other purposes approved by the Commissioners of Customs and Excise. In the event of the Society being dissolved through inability to meet its financial obligations all Voting Members excluding Life Members shall contribute their share of the deficiency.
6 The Officers of the Society shall consist of President, Vice-President, Secretary, Assistant Secretary, Business Manager, Treasurer, Publicity Manager, all of whom shall be elected annually and all of whom shall have power to vote. The Socials Committee Secretary, Honorary Members' Secretary and Ticket Secretary shall also be elected annually but shall not have power to vote by virtue of the office.
The business of the Society shall be vested in a Committee of Active Members to be known as the General Management Committee consisting of the Business Manager, Treasurer, Secretary, Assistant Secretary, Publicity Manager, and six other Active Members, with power to add to their number, five to form a quorum. The Chairman of the Social Committee shall be a member of the General Management Committee and appointed by that body. The six elected Active Members shall serve for two years, three members retiring annually, but shall be elegible for re-election. In the event of equality of service upon the Committee the order of retirement, unless agreed between the parties concerned, shall be by ballot.
8 The General Management Committee shall have power to appoint sub-committees as they shall deem necessary. The decisions of any sub-Committee shall be subject to the approval of the General Management Committee.
9 Any member of the General Management Committee, or of any other Committee appointed at the Annual General Meeting, being absent from three consecutive meetings without giving a satisfactory reason, shall be compelled to resign and the vacancy shall be filled by the General Management Committee. No member serving on the General Management Committee of any other Operatic Society shall be eligible for election to the General Management Committee.
10 The General Management Committee shall decide the shows to be produced and shall appoint a Producer, Musical Director and Choreographer for each production.
11 A Socials Committee, consisting of six members, shall be elected at the Annual General Meeting, and they shall be responsible for the Social Activities of the Society. They shall keep their own accounts, which shall be submitted to the Auditors, but shall not incur any liability in the name of the Society without the sanction of the General Management Committee. The Socials Committee may fill any casual vacancy or co-opt other members.
12 Applications for admission to active membership of the Society shall be dealt with by the General Management Committee. This Committee shall also have power to admit Associate Members, with or without subscription, for such period as they think fit. Such Associate Members shall have the same status as Active Members but shall not be entitled to take part in any production except at the express invitation of the General Management Committee.
13 The Cast for any production shall be selected by a Selection Committee which shall consist of:
   (*a*) The Chairman of the General Management Committee who shall be the Chairman of the Selection Committee and shall exercise only a casting vote.
   (*b*) Two persons (other than Active Members) selected by the General Management Committee for their knowledge and experience.
   (*c*) One member of the General Management Committee elected by that Committee.
   (*d*) Two active members elected by members of the Society.
   (*e*) Producer, Musical Director and Choreographer.

Five members of the Selection Committee shall form a quorum. The Secretary or Assistant Secretary shall attend ex-officio. The General Management Committee shall have power to fill any parts not cast by the Selection Committee, to revise the cast from time to time if any member to whom a part has been assigned shall, in its opinion, prove unsuitable for the part, and to re-cast any part becoming vacant for any reason whatsoever.

14 The General Management Committee shall appoint a Special Committee for the selection of Dancers, consisting of such persons as they may think suitable.

15 (a) Every Active Member of the Society shall pay such Annual Subscription as shall be decided at each Annual General Meeting. This subscription will become due on 1st June and payment must be completed by 1st November. Members shall provide their own music and libretto for each production.
(b) Any Active Member failing to pay his or her subscription by 1st November shall not take part in any of the Society's activities except at the discretion of the General Management Committee.
(c) Persons admitted for their dancing ability only shall pay such subscription as the General Management Committee shall decide.

16 Honorary Members may be admitted to the Society at the discretion of the General Management Committee on payment of an Annual Subscription of 15/– due on 1st June, and they shall be entitled to a rebate of 5/– on one ticket for each operatic production, provided the Annual Subscription is paid before the date of the first show. Honorary Members shall not be entitled to vote at General Meetings, but may be heard on any subject under discussion.

17 Members taking tickets for productions are responsible for payment if such tickets are not returned to the Ticket Secretary at least SEVEN clear days prior to the first performance.

18 Rehearsals shall be held on every Monday and Thursday at 7.30 p.m. prompt, at Bounds Green School, or at such other times and places as the General Management Committee shall deem advisable.

19 Members shall attend the authentic rehearsals of the Society punctually and regularly and any member disregarding this rule will be liable to be placed on the reserve, after caution by the Committee.

20 A statement showing the financial result of the production shall be prepared and presented to the Society not later than one month after each production and Accounts for the financial year ended 31st May in each year shall be prepared and audited and presented to the Society at the Annual General Meeting which shall be held as soon as possible after that date.

21 An Extraordinary General Meeting of the Society may be called at any time at the discretion of the General Management Committee by giving seven days' notice to the Members of the Society. Such meeting shall also be called within twenty-one days after receipt by the Secretary of a requisition signed by at least twelve Active Members of the Society. Any such requisition shall specify the business for which the meeting is to be convened and no other business shall be transacted at that Meeting. No business other than the formal adjournment of the meeting shall be transacted at any General Meeting unless a quorum be present and such quorum shall consist of not less than twenty persons present and entitled to vote.

22 All Resolutions to be moved at a General Meeting shall be sent to the Secretary, together with the name of the Proposer, at least twenty-one days before the meeting.

23 All new rules and amendments to rules must be voted for by two-thirds of those attending the Meeting and entitled to vote before they can be incorporated in the Society's Book of Rules.

24 Any matter not provided for in the foregoing rules shall be left to the discretion of the General Management Committee.

DIRECTORY OF SHOWS, SUPPLIERS AND SERVICES

Part A is a comprehensive list of musical shows available for amateur performances, listed alphabetically by title, and giving the names of the composer and the copyright holders.
Part B is a list of various suppliers of theatrical equipment and services, listed alphabetically under various headings.

Every effort has been made to ensure that the details given in this directory are correct at time of going to press, but with the current introduction of STD and the allocation of new telephone numbers, it may be desirable to check the telephone numbers listed with the exchange before making a call.

The copyright owners should be contacted before a show is decided upon, in order to ascertain whether the amateur performing rights will be available at the time of the production.

PART A

Addresses of copyright owners

Ascherberg	Ascherberg, Hopwood & Crew Ltd, 16 Mortimer Street, London, W.1. (MUSeum 3562)
Barrington	Clarence Barrington, 180 Wyndora Avenue, Harbord, N.S.W., Australia.
Boosey	Boosey & Hawkes, Ltd, 295 Regent Street, London, W.1. (LANgham 2060)
Brentfield	Brentfield Enterprises, 147 Banks Road, Sandbanks, Poole, Dorset.
Chappell	Chappell & Co. Ltd, 50 New Bond Street, London, W.1. (MAYfair 7600)
Cramer	J. B. Cramer & Co. Ltd, 99 St. Martin's Lane, London, W.C.2. (COVent Garden 1612)
Curwen	J. Curwen & Sons, Ltd, 29 Maiden Lane, London, W.C.2. (COVent Garden 1666)
Dance	George Dance Musical Plays, 63 Piccadilly, London, W.1. (HYDe Park 2552)
Evans	Evans Bros. Ltd, Montague House, Russell Square, London, W.C.1. (MUSeum 8521)
French	Samuel French Ltd, 26 Southampton Street, London, W.C.2. (TEMple Bar 7513)
Glocken Verlag	Glocken Verlag, Ltd, 10-16 Rathbone Street, London, W.1. (01 580 2827)
Littler	Emile Littler Musical Play Dept, Palace Theatre, Shaftesbury Avenue, London, W.1. (GERrard 3890)
M & Y	Macdonald & Young, Emanwye House, Bernard Street, London, W.C.1. (TERminus 6217)
Noda	Noda Ltd, 1 Crestfield Street, London, W.C.1. (TERminus 5655)
Pladio	Pladio Ltd, 22 Upper Brook Street, London, W.1. (GROsvenor 5333)
Prowse	Keith Prowse Music Publishing Co. Ltd, 21 Denmark Street, London, W.C.2. (TEMple Bar 3856)
Weinberger	Josef Weinberger Ltd, 10-16 Rathbone Street, London, W.1. (01 580 2827)
Williams	Joseph Williams Ltd, 148 Charing Cross Road, London, W.C.2. (TEMple Bar 3694)

Title	*Composer*	*Copyright owners (or controllers of performing rights)*
After the Ball	Noel Coward	French
Andrea Chenier	Giordano	Ascherberg
Andriana Le Couvreur	Cilea	Ascherberg
And So To Bed	Vivian Ellis	French
Annie Get Your Gun	Irving Berlin	Littler
Anything Goes	Cole Porter	French
Arcadians, The	Monckton and Talbot	French
Baker Street	Grudeff and Jessel	Noda
Balalaika	Posford and Green	French
Balkan Princess, The	Rubens	Dance
Bartered Bride, The	Smetana	Boosey & Hawkes
Beach Girl	Barrington	Barrington
Beggar's Opera, The	Austin	Boosey
Beggar Student, The	Milloecker	Weinberger
Belinda Fair	Strachey	French

Belle of New York, The	Kerker	French
Bells are Ringing	Styne	Chappell
Betty	Rubens	Littler
Bitter Sweet	Coward	French
Bird Seller, The	Zeller	Weinberger
Bless the Bride	Ellis	French
Blossom Time	Schubert-Clutsam	French
Blue For A Boy	Parr Davies	Littler
Bob's Your Uncle	Gay	French
Bohemian Girl	Balfe	No performing fee
Boy, The	Bereny	Littler
Boy Friend, The	Wilson	French
Brigadoon	Loewe	Chappell
Bye Bye Birdie	Strouse	Chappell
Cabaret Girl, A	Kern	Littler
Calamity Jane	Fain	Weinberger
Call Me Madam	Berlin	Chappell
Camelot	Loewe	Chappell
Can-Can	Porter	Noda
Careless Rapture	Novello	French
Carissima	May	French
Carmen	Bizet	Cramer
Carousel	Rodgers	Chappell
Castles in Spain	Brae	French
Cathine	Tschaikowsky	Littler
Cavalleria Rusticana	Mascagni	Ascherberg
Chrysanthemum	Stewart	French
Chu Chin Chow	Norton	French
Cindy	Brandon	Noda
Circus Girl, The	Caryll and Monckton	Littler
Cloches de Corneville, Les	Planquette	Williams
Count of Luxembourg	Lehar-Grun	Glocken Verlag
Count of Luxembourg	Lehar-Hood-Ross	Littler
Country Girl, A	Monckton	Littler
Cox and Box	Sullivan	No performing fee
Damask Rose	Chopin	M and Y
Dancing Mistress, The	Monckton	Littler
Dancing Years, The	Novello	French
Dear Miss Phoebe	Parr-Davies	Littler
Desert Song, The	Romberg	French
Destry Rides Again	Rome	Noda
Dick Turpin	Brooks	Weinberger
Die Fledermaus	Strauss-Hanmer	Weinberger
Dorothy	Cellier	Chappell
Down in the Valley	Kurt Weill	Schirmer
Dubarry, The	Milloecker	French
Duchess of Dantzig, The	Caryll	Littler
Duenna, The	Slade	French
Emerald Isle, The	Sullivan and German	Chappell
Engaged! Or Cheviot's Choice	Sullivan	Chappell
Expresso Bongo	Heneker and Norman	Evans
Fade Out—Fade In	Styne	Noda
Fantasticks, The	Schmidt	Chappell
Finian's Rainbow	Lane	Chappell
Florodora	Stuart	Noda
Flower Drum Song	Rodgers	Chappell
Free As Air	Slade	French
Funny Girl	Styne	Noda
Funny Thing Happened on the Way to The Forum, A	Sondheim	Chappell
Gay's The Word	Novello	French
Geisha, The	Jones	Littler
Gipsy Baron, The	Strauss-Hanmer	Weinberger
Gipsy Love	Lehar-Hanmer	Glocken Verlag
Gipsy Love	Lehar-Hood-Ross	Littler
Gipsy Princess, The	Kalman-Hanmer	Weinberger
Girl Friend, The	Rodgers	M and Y
Girl From Utah, The	Jones and Rubens	Littler

Girls of Gothenburg, The	Caryll and Monckton	Littler
Glamorous Night	Novello	French
Golden City	Tore	French
Gondoliers, The	Sullivan	No performing fee
Goodnight Vienna	Posford	French
Grab Me a Gondola	James Gilbert	Littler
Grand Duchess, The	Offenbach	Boosey and Hawkes
Grand Duke, The	Sullivan	No performing fee
Guys and Dolls	Loesser	Chappell
HMS Pinafore	Sullivan	No performing fee
Haddon Hall	Sullivan	No performing fee
Half a Sixpence	Heneker	Chappell
Half in Ernest	Ellis	Chappell
Harmony Hill	Glass	Noda
Havana	Stuart	Littler
High Button Shoes	Styne	Noda
Highwayman Love	Bullock	Curwen
Hit the Deck	Youmans	M and Y
How to Succeed in Business		
without Really Trying	Loesser	Chappell
Hugh the Drover	Vaughan Williams	Curwen
Iolanthe	Sullivan	No performing fee
Irene	Tierney	M and Y
Irma la Douce	Monnot	Chappell
Jill Darling	Ellis	French
Jolly Roger	Leigh	Boosey
Katinka	Friml	M and Y
King and I, The	Rodgers	Chappell
King's Rhapsody	Novello	French
Kismet	Borodin-Wright-Forrest	French
Kiss Me Kate	Porter	Noda
La Belle Helene	Offenbach-Hanmer	Weinberger
Lady Be Good	Gershwin	M and Y
Lady of the Rose, The	Jean Gilbert	Littler
L'Amico Fritz	Mascagni	Ascherberg
Land of Smiles, The	Lehar	Glocken Verlag
Last Waltz, The	Oscar Strauss	Littler
Let's Make An Opera	Britten	Boosey
Lilac Domino, The	Cuvillier	M and Y
Lilac Time	Schubert-Clutsam	Chappell
Lily of Killarney	Benedict	No performing fee
Lisbon Story, The	Parr Davies	Chappell
Little Mary Sunshine	Besoyan	French
Little Me	Coleman	Noda
Little Nelly Kelly	Cohan	Littler
Lock up your Daughters	Johnson	French
Love at the Inn	Quilter	Ascherberg
Love from Judy	Martin	Littler
Madame Pompadour	Fall	Littler
Magyar Melody	Posford and Grun	French
Maid of the Mountains, The	Fraser Simson	Littler
Make me an Offer	Heneker and Norman	French
Maritza	Kalman	French
Marriage Market, The	Jacobi	Littler
Masquerade	Posford	French
Me and My Girl	Gay	French
Meet me by Moonlight	Traditional	Evans
Mercenary Mary	Friedlander and Conrad	M and Y
Merchant Prince	Sterling Hill	Noda
Merrie England	German	Chappell
Merrie England	German-Arundel	Chappell
Merry Widow	Lehar	Glocken Verlag
Mikado, The	Sullivan	No performing fee
Millions Buy It	Blomfield and Brent	Brentfield
Miss Hook of Holland	Rubens	Littler
Mr Cinders	Ellis and Myers	M and Y
Mr Pepys	Shaw	French
Monsieur Beaucaire	Messager	Ascherberg

Most Happy Fella, The	Loesser	Chappell
Mousmé, The	Monckton and Talbot	M and Y
Music in the Air	Kern	Chappell
Music Man, The	Willson	Chappell
My Fair Lady	Loewe	Chappell
Naughty Marietta	Herbert	Weinberger
New Moon, The	Romberg	Chappell
Night in Venice	Johann Strauss-May	Weinberger
Nina Rosa	Romberg	French
No, No, Nanette	Youmans	French
Oh Captain!	Livingston and Evans	Noda
Oh, Oh Delphine	Caryll	M and Y
Old Chelsea	Tauber-Grun	French
Oliver	Bart	Noda
Oklahoma!	Rodgers	Chappell
O Marry Me!	Kessler	Chappell
Orpheus in the Underworld	Offenbach-Hanmer	Weinberger
Our Miss Gibbs	Caryll and Monckton	Littler
Over She Goes	Mayerl	Noda
Paganini	Lehar	Glocken Verlag
Pagliacci	Leoncavallo	Ascherberg
Paint your Wagon	Loewe	Chappell
Pajama Game, The	Adler and Ross	Chappell
Paris in the Spring	Markham Lee	Curwen
Passion Flower	Bizet-Grun	Prowse
Patience	Sullivan	No performing fee
Paul Jones	Planquette	Ascherberg
Penelope Anne	Le Fleming	M and Y
Perchance to Dream	Novello	French
Pink Champagne	Johann Strauss-Grun	French
Pirates of Penzance, The	Sullivan	No performing fee
Please Teacher	Waller and Tunbridge	M and Y
Primrose	Gershwin	Littler
Princess Charming	Sirmay	M and Y
Princess Ida	Sullivan	No performing fee
Princess of Kensington, A	German	Chappell
Quaker Girl, The	Monckton	Littler
Rainbow Inn	Strong	French
Rebel Maid, The	Phillips	Chappell
Red Mill, The	Herbert	Noda
Rio Rita	Tierney	French
Roar of the Grease Paint— Smell of the Crowd	Bricusse and Newley	Noda
Rose Marie	Friml and Stothart	French
Rose of Persia	Sullivan	No performing fee
Ruddigore	Sullivan	No performing fee
Runaway Girl, A	Caryll and Monckton	Littler
Salad Days	Slade	French
Sally	Kern	Littler
San Toy	Jones	Littler
Shop Girl, The	Caryll, Ross and Monckton	Littler
Show Boat	Kern	Chappell
Song of Norway	Grieg	Chappell
Sorcerer, The	Sullivan	No performing fee
Southern Maid	Fraser-Simson	Littler
South Pacific	Rodgers	Chappell
Stop the World—I Want To Get Off	Bricusse and Newley	Noda
Street Scene	Weill	Chappell
Street Singer, The	Fraser-Simson	French
Student Love	Brahms, arr. Spurgin	French
Student Prince	Romberg	Pladio
Summer Song	Dvorak-Grun	French
Sunny	Kern	Chappell
Sweethearts	Herbert	Weinberger
Sweet Yesterday	Leslie-Smith	French
Sybil	Jacobi	Littler
Tantivy Towers	Dunhill	Cramer

Tell Me More	Gershwin	Littler
1066—And All That	Reynolds	French
There and Back	Sullivan/Leigh	Noda
Three Musketeers, The	Friml	Chappell
Tina	Rubens and Haydn Wood	Littler
Tom Jones	German	Chappell
Tonight's the Night	Rubens	Littler
Toreador, The	Caryll and Monckton	Littler
Trial by Jury	Sullivan	No performing fee
Tulip Time	Wark	French
Two Bouquets	Irving	French
Utopia Limited	Sullivan	No performing fee
Vagabond King, The	Friml	French
Valley of Song	Novello	Weinberger
Veronique	Messager	Littler
Vie Parisienne, La	Offenbach	Boosey
Viktoria and her Hussar	Abraham	French
Virginia	Waller and Tunbridge	M and Y
Waltz Dream, A	Oscar Straus	Littler
Waltz Time	May	M and Y
Waltz Without End	Chopin-Grun	French
Waltzes from Vienna	Johann Strauss-Hanmer	Weinberger
Water Gipsies	Ellis	French
Wedding in Paris	May	French
West Side Story	Bernstein	Chappell
Where's Charley?	Loesser	French
White Horse Inn	Benatzky and Stoltz	French
Who's Hooper!	Talbot and Novello	Littler
Wild Grows the Heather	Waller and Tunbridge	French
Wildflower	Stothart and Youmans	Pladio
Wild Violets	Stolz	Chappell
Wizard of Oz	Braun, Harburg and Arlen	Weinberger
Wonderful Town	Bernstein	Noda
Yeoman of the Guard	Sullivan	No performing fee
Zip Goes a Million	Posford	Littler

PART B

COSTUMES

Charles Alty	57 Aughton Street, Ormskirk, Lancs. (Aughton Green 3318)
Morris Angel & Son Ltd	117/9 Shaftesbury Avenue, London, W.C.2. (TEMple Bar 5678)
Arena Theatre Studios	Marston Road, Sutton Coldfield. (Erdington 1961, 1288)
M. Berman, Ltd	18 Irving Street, London, W.C.2. (TRAfalgar 1651/9)
Berman's Revue (Costumes) Ltd	16 Orange Street, London, W.C.2. (TRAfalgar 1530)
Black Lion Costumes	25 Summerville Road, Bristol 7. (Bristol 41345)
Bonn & Mackenzie Ltd	24 Betterton Street, London, W.C.2. (TEmple Bar 1393)
Bristol Old Vic Wardrobe Hire	Colston House, Bristol.
A. & L. Corne Ltd	3 Tanner Street, London, S.E.1. (HOP 3451)
Costume Studio	87 Harnham Road, Salisbury, Wilts. (Salisbury 4351)
Richard Dendy & Associates	2 Aultone Yard, Carshalton, Surrey. (WALlington 8765)
Eltham Little Theatre	Wythfield Road, London, S.E.9. (ELTham 3702)
Chas. H. Fox Ltd	184 High Holborn, London, W.C.1. (HOLborn 9557)
W. A. Homburg Ltd	31 Call Lane, Leeds 1. (Leeds 28425)
Louise	3 Ryehill Grove, Hull, Yorks. (Hull 77053)
M. & J. Luxton	32 Kensington Park Road, London, W.11. (PARk 7912)

Lyndon Hire Service	16–20 Hamlet Court Road, Westcliff-on-Sea, Essex. (Southend-on-Sea 42964)
Masque Costumes	72 Tenbury Road, Birmingham, 14.
C. & W. May Ltd	9 Garrick Street, London, W.C.2. (TEMple Bar 6525)
Moss Bros. & Co. Ltd	20 King Street, London, W.C.2. (TEMple Bar 4477)
Mountview Theatre Club	104 Crouch Hill, London, N.8. (MOUntview 5885)
William Mutrie & Son Ltd	Proscenium House, Broughton Street, Edinburgh 1. (Edinburgh-Waverley 6424/5)
L. & H. Nathan Ltd	143 Drury Lane, London, W.C.2. (TEMple Bar 3671)
Louise Newell	3 Ryehill Grove, Preston Road, Hull. (Hull 77053)
Old Vic Theatre	Waterloo Road, London, S.E.1. (WATerloo 4871)
James Parker Ltd (theatre costumes)	21/2 Poland Street, London, W.1. (GERrard 6315)
Pantomime House	Cozells Street, Birmingham, 1. (MIDland 7475)
M. Prager Ltd	6 St. Cuthbert's Road, London, N.W.2. (GLAdstone 2828)
Sign of Four	7 Derby Road, Nottingham. (Nottingham 44177)
Alec Shanks (stage costumes) Ltd	18 Garrick Street, London, W.C.2. (COVent Garden 1489)
Nellie Smith	190 Mansfield Road, Nottingham. (Nottingham 64452)
Sally Spruce	49 Greek Street, London, W.1. (GERrard 3162)
Stage Furnishings Ltd	346 Sauchiehall Street, Glasgow, C.2. (DOUglas 6431/2)
Star Scenic Studios	78 Elms Road, London, S.W.4. (MACaulay 6401/2)
Frank Stuart	3 Medway Court, Leigh Street, London, W.C.1. (EUSton 2314)
Tavistock Repertory Company	Tower Theatre, Canonbury Place, London, N.1. (CANonbury 5111)
Theatre Workshop	Theatre Royal, Stratford, London, E.13. (MARyland 5973)
Theatre Zoo	28 New Row, St. Martin's Lane, London, W.C.2. (TEMple Bar 3150)
S. B. Watts & Co.	18/20 New Brown Street, Manchester 4. (Manchester, Blackfriars 5826/7)
Wilmslow Guild	1 Boulne Street, Wilmslow, Cheshire.
Young's Dress Hire Ltd	178/180 Wardour Street, London, W.1. (GERrard 4422)

FURNITURE AND FURNISHINGS

Arena Theatre Studios	Marston Road, Sutton Coldfield. (Erdington 1961 1288)
Connoisseur	528 Wilmslow Road, Manchester 20. (Didsbury 2504)
C. Crosdale	477 Barlow Moor Road, Manchester 21. (Charlton 5117)
Gimbert's Ltd	Cedar Avenue, Whitefield, Manchester. (Whitefield 2076)
Old Times Furnishing Co.	135 Lower Richmond Road, London, S.W.15. (PUTney 3551)
Pantomime House	Oozells Street, Birmingham, 1. (MIDland 7475)

LIGHTING EQUIPMENT

W. J. Furse and Co. Ltd	22 Alie Street, London, E.1. (ROYal 9041/5)
John Griffin Theatre Studio	175 Wollaton Street, Nottingham. (Nottingham 43623)
J.M.B. Hire Co. Ltd	87 Lamb's Conduit Street, London, W.C.1. (HOLborn 6546 CHAncery 2205)
Major Equipment Co. Ltd	22 Gorst Road, London, N.W.10. (ELGar 8041). Sale only.
Rank Audio Visual Ltd	Woodger Road, London, W.12. (SHEpherds Bush 2050). Sale only.

Strand Electric & Engineering Co. Ltd	29 King Street, London, W.C.2. (TEMple Bar 4444)
Hire Dept and Fittings	271 Kennington Lane, London, S.E.11. (RELiance 7811)
Manchester	313–317 Oldham Road, Manchester 10. (Collyhurst 2736)
Darlington	3 Kemble Green North, Newton Aycliffe, Darlington. (Newton Aycliffe 593)
Bristol	56 Fouracre Crescent, Downend, Bristol. (Bristol 651460)
Dublin	30 Upper Abbey Street, Dublin. (Dublin 47078)
Scotland	Stage Furnishings Ltd, 346 Sauchiehall Street, Glasgow, C.2. (Douglas 6431)
Australia	212 Graham Street, Port Melbourne, Victoria. (64-1267)
Canada	261 Davenport Road, Toronto 5, Ontario. (925-5108)
Theatre Projects (Lighting) Ltd	5 Goodwin's Court, St. Martin's Lane, London, W.C.2. (TEMple Bar 7879)
Theatre Lights Hire Co.	31 Preston Road, Lytham St. Annes, Lancs. (Lytham 6112)

MAKE-UP

Anello & Davide	96 Charing Cross Road, London, W.C.2. (TEMple Bar 5019)
'Bert'	46 Portnall Road, London, W.9. (LADbroke 1717)
Max Factor, Hollywood & London (Sales) Ltd	16 Old Bond Street, London, W.1. (HYDe Park 6720)
Chas. H. Fox Ltd	184 High Holborn, London, W.C.1. (HOLborn 9557)
Samuel French Ltd	26 Southampton Street, London, W.C.2. (TEMple Bar 7513)
C. A. W. Holmes	(Make-up artist), 46 Lansdowne Road, London, N.17. (TOTtenham 2315)
L. Leichner (London) Ltd	(Studio), 44a Cranbourn Street, London, W.C.2. (REGent 7166/8)
William Mutrie & Son Ltd	Proscenium House, Broughton Street, Edinburgh 1. (Edinburgh 34663)
Sign of Four	7 Derby Road, Nottingham. (Nottingham 44177)
Nellie Smith	190 Mansfield Road, Nottingham. (Nottingham 64452)
J. H. Spaans	7 Lisle Street, London, W.C.2. (GERrard 4071)
Stage Furnishings Ltd	346 Sauchiehall Street, Glasgow, C.2. (Douglas 6431/2)

PROPERTIES FOR HIRE
(General props for sale or hire unless otherwise indicated)

Bapty & Co.	39 Whitcomb Street, London, W.C.2. (930-6541). Weapons and firearms.
Barnum's Carnival Novelties	67 Hammersmith Road, London, W.14. (FULham 4440)
Cape Scenic Service	85 Crouch Hill, London, N.8. (ARChway 4654)
Richard Dendy & Associates	2 Aulton Yard, Carshalton, Surrey. (WALlington 8765)
Dramaprops	20 Bush Hill Road, London, N.21. (LABurnum 6514 PALmers Green 9842, 4208). Properties made to order.
Floral Decor	15 Gerrard Street, London, W.1. (GERrard 1957). Flowers.
Edward Gerrard & Sons	61 College Place, London, N.W.1. (EUSton 2765). Stuffed animals, birds, skins.
Gimbert's Limited	Cedar Avenue, Whitefield, Manchester. (Whitefield 2076)
Jewelcraft	1 Argyll Street, London, W.1. (GERrard 4047)
Louise	3 Ryehill Grove, Hull, Yorks. (Hull 77053)
Maximes Studio	Bloomsbury Hall, All Saints, Manchester. (Ardwick 2796). Props and animal skins.
J. George Morley	56 Old Brompton Road, London, S.W.7. (KENsington 4743). Antique musical instruments.
Mountview Theatre Club	104 Crouch Hill, London, N.8. (MOUntview 5885)
Old Times Furnishing Co.	135 Lower Richmond Road, London, S.W.15. (PUTney 3551)
A. Robinson & Son Ltd	47 Monmouth Street, London, W.C.2. (COVent Garden 0110)
Sign of Four	7 Derby Road, Nottingham. (Nottingham 44177)
Stage-Decor Ltd	The Browning Hall, Browning Street, S.E.17. (RODney 4771)
Stage Properties Ltd	12 Orange Street, London, W.C.2. (930-8528)
Star Scenic Studios	78 Elms Road, London, S.W.4. (MACaulay 6401/2)
Studio & TV Hire Ltd	30 John Islip Street, London, S.W.1. (VICtoria 9996)
Frank Stuart	3 Medway Court, Leight Street, London, W.C.1. (EUSton 2314). Masks, cane work.
Theatre Studios Ltd	2 Neals Yard, Monmouth Street, London, W.C.2. (TEMple Bar 5574). Sculpture and special props.
Theatre Zoo	28 New Row, St. Martin's Lane, London, W.C.2. (TEMple Bar 3150). Heads, masks and unusual props.
Robert White & Sons	57/59 Neal Street, London, W.C.2. (TEMple Bar 8237). Armour, swords, jewellery.

SCENERY FOR SALE AND HIRE

E. Babbage & Co. Ltd	1–5 Andrew Place, Cowthorpe Road, London, S.W.8. (MACaulay 5818)
Brunskill & Loveday Ltd	1–3 Newport Street, London, S.E.11. (RELiance 1518, 1988). Sale only.
Cape Scenic Service	85 Crouch Hill, London, N.8. (ARChway 4654)
Trevor Cresswell Organisation	Facing Drill Hall, Bury, Lancs. (Bury 3227)
Dodsword & Spencer	Wellington Road Studio, Undercliffe, Bradford 2. (Bradford 37137)
Empire Scenic Studios	St. Paul's Road, Smethwick, Staffs. (Smethwick 1100)
Festival Workshop	Midland Bank Chambers, Welwyn Garden City, Herts. Scenery made to order. Rostra for hire or sale.
James Fredericks	Scenic Studios, Langford Road, Weston-super-Mare. (Weston-super-Mare 4791)
Joan Griffin & Co.	The Studio, 49–55 Denison Street, Alfreton Road, Nottingham. (Nottingham 247215)
Heather Studios	76c Bingley Road, Saltaire, Shipley, Yorks. (Ilkley 1088 Shipley 51842)
Mara & Houghton	Kings Cross Goods Depot, York Way, London, N.1. (TERminus 5181)
Victor Mara Ltd	72a Plough Road, London, S.W.11. (BATtersea 7337). Scenery builders.
Maximes Studio	*Head Office:* 26 Penrose Avenue, Blackpool, Lancs. (Blackpool 62861) *Studio:* King Street, Haslingden, Lancs. (Rossendale 4950)
Midland Stage Decor	c/o Robert Weaver, 21 Northvale Close, Kenilworth, Warwickshire.
William Mutrie & Son Ltd	Proscenium House, Broughton Street, Edinburgh 1. (Edinburgh 34663)
Russell & Chapple Ltd	23 Monmouth Street, London, W.C.2. (TEMple Bar 7521)
Scenic Display Services Ltd	Norcroft Studios, Listerhills Road, Bradford 7. (Bradford 24377). Sale only.
Stage Furnishings Limited	346 Sauchiehall Street, Glasgow, C.2. (Douglas 6431/2)
Stage Productions Limited	The Hall, Camden Park Road, London, N.W.1. (GULliver 3309)
Star Scenic Studios	78 Elms Road, London, S.W.4. (MACaulay 6401/2)
Watts & Corry Limited	305/317 Oldham Road, Manchester 10. (Collyhurst 2736)
A. Whyatt & Son	Hartley Street, Wolverhampton.

SCENIC MATERIALS

Brodie & Middleton Ltd	79 Long Acre, London, W.C.2. (TEMple Bar 3280, 3289)
B. Burnet & Co. Limited	22 Garrick Street, London, W.C.2. (TEMple Bar 3972, 4893)
I. L. Davies	32 Jews Row, London, S.W.18.
Samuel French Ltd	26 Southampton Street, London, W.C.2. (TEMple Bar 7513)
Hamilton & Hargraves Ltd	5 New Brown Street, Manchester 4.
John Holliday & Sons Ltd	12 Little Britain, London, E.C.1. (METropolitan 0515). Curtains, draperies.
Rex Howard	12 Connaught Street, London, W.2. (PADdington 3600). Curtains, drapes.
A. Leete & Co. (Sales) Ltd	129/130 London Road, London, S.E.1. (WATerloo 5283)
Russell & Chapple Ltd	23 Monmouth Street, London, W.C.2. (TEMple Bar 7521)
G. W. Scott & Sons	4 Tower Street, London, W.C.2. (TEMple Bar 0153). 'Wrought iron' balustrades (made from cane).
Star Scenic Studios	78 Elms Road, London, S.W.4. (MACaulay 6401/2)
Watts & Corry Ltd	305/317 Oldham Road, Manchester 10. (Collyhurst 2736)

EFFECTS

Barnum's Carnival Novelties	67 Hammersmith Road, London, W.14. (FULham 4440, 4448)
Bishop Sound & Electrical Co. Ltd	48 Monmouth Street, London, W.C.2. (TEMple Bar 7484/5). Effects records for sale.
Lewis Davenport & Co.	51 Great Russell Street, London, W.C.1. (HOLborn 8524). Tricks.
Richard Dendy & Associates	2 Aultone Yard, Carshalton, Surrey. (WALlington 8765). Smoke and mist machines for hire.
E.M.I. Studios Ltd	20 Manchester Square, London, W.1. (HUNter 4488). Effects records for sale.
L. W. Hunt Drum Co.	10 Archer Street, London, W.1. (GERrard 8911/3). Effects machines for sale or hire.

KLP Film Services Ltd	3 Queens Crescent, Richmond, Surrey. Sound effects on tape.
Microsound	70 Nursery Road, Cheadle Hulme, Cheshire. (Hulme Hall 4681). Effects on disc or tape.
Pye Records Ltd	ATV House, Great Cumberland Place, London, W.1. (AMBassador 5502)
Rumney Gibson Ltd	St. Ann's Road, Harrow. Fog and smoke effects.
Stagesound (London) Ltd	11/12 King Street, London, W.C.2. (COVent Garden 0955). Effects records for sale.
Strand Electric and Engineering Co. Ltd	29 King Street, London, W.C.2. (TEMple Bar 4444). Electrical effects and pyrotechnics. See under 'Lighting' for full list of addresses.

WIGS FOR SALE AND HIRE

'Bert'	46 Portrall Road, London, W.9. (LADbroke 1717)
Chas. H. Fox Ltd	184 High Holborn, London, W.C.1. (HOLborn 9557)
W. A. Homburg Ltd	31 Call Lane, Leeds 1. (Leeds 28425)
W. A. Hume & Sons	88–94 Oxford Street, Manchester 1. (Central 2244)
William Mutrie & Son Ltd	Proscenium House, Broughton Street, Edinburgh 1. (Edinburgh 34663)
Nathanwigs Ltd	143 Drury Lane, London, W.C.2. (TEMple Bar 3671)
Sign of Four	7 Derby Road, Nottingham. (Nottingham 44177)
Nellie Smith	190 Mansfield Road, Nottingham. (Nottingham 64452)
J. H. Spaans	7 Lisle Street, London, W.C.2. (GERrard 4071)
Wig Creations Ltd	22 Portman Close, London, W.1. (HUNter 0771)
Wig Specialities Ltd	173 Seymour Place, London, W.1. (AMBassador 6565)
Wrathbaron & Co.	Ravenshill, Sutton, Keighley, Yorks.

MISCELLANEOUS SUPPLIES

Caledonian Insurance Co.	(Official insurers appointed by Noda), 51 King Street, Manchester 2. (Deansgate 5626)
Creative Printing & Advertising Co. Ltd	Ponsharden, Falmouth, Cornwall.
Eugene's Flying Ballets	12 Barons Court Mansions, Gledstanes Road, London, W.14. (FULham 8172)
Kirby's Flying Ballet	10 Berriedale Avenue, Hove 3, Sussex. (Hove 37133)
Lusby & Pollard Ltd	Bradford Road, Stanningley, Nr. Leeds. Hampers.
National Operatic & Dramatic Association	1 Crestfield Street, London, W.C.1. (TERminus 5655)
Benjamin Pollock Ltd	44 Monmouth Street, London, W.C.2. (COVent Garden 2369). Toy theatres.
Rex Thomas (Insurance) Ltd	(Official brokers to British Drama League), 354 Ballards Lane, London, N.12. (HILlside 6373/6)
Theatres Mutual Insurance Co. Ltd	79 Pall Mall, London, S.W.1. (WHItehall 4422) 131 St. Vincent Street, Glasgow, C.2. 17 Park Row, Leeds 1. 30 Cross Street, Manchester 2.
W. Vandervelde	4 Newman Passage, London, W.1. Skips, wardrobes, trunks.

GLOSSARY

ACT DROP	A painted cloth or curtain that can be lowered at the end of each act.
ACTING AREA	That part of the stage whereon the action of the play takes place.
APRON	The extension of the stage projecting in front of the proscenium arch. Also referred to as 'apron stage' or 'fore-stage'.
A.S.M.	Assistant stage manager.
AT RISE	The stage when ready for the rise of the curtain.
AUDITORIUM	The part of the theatre where the audience is seated to watch the performance.
BACKDROP (BACKCLOTH)	A curtain, or painted canvas sheet, battened top and bottom and hung on a set of lines across the back of a scene.
BACKING	Scenery used behind openings (e.g. windows or doors) to limit the audience's view.
BAND ROOM	A room, usually under the stage, used by the orchestra.
BARREL	Length of metal pipe suspended on a set of lines. Usually found in the counterweight system.
BATTEN	(a) A length of timber or pipe, suspended from a set of lines, to which scenery is attached for flying.

	(*b*) A length of timber used to stiffen a hanging cloth at its lower edge.
	(*c*) Any length of wood used in scenery construction.
	(*d*) A length of metal troughing carrying lamps and suspended over and lighting the acting area.
BOAT TRUCK	Low free-moving trolley on which scneery can be pre-set for quick changes.
BOBBIN	Cylindrical carrier for drawing curtains on a horizontal track.
BOOK-CEILING	A hinged ceiling piece (rarely used in musicals).
BOOK-FLAT	A pair of hinged flats.
BOOK-WING	Constructed and set as a bookflat. Often used in exteriors.
BORDER	A strip of canvas suspended from above and used to mask the upper part of the stage, and the lanterns. Often painted to represent foliage or sky. They are numbered from one upwards, starting at the proscenium arch. Current practice in certain West End shows is to ignore the question of masking above the stage and to leave the equipment in view of the audience.
BOX SET	A series of flats, joined together to make an interior scene.
BRACE	(*a*) Piece of wood, inserted diagonally into the frame of a flat to strengthen it.
	(*b*) An adjustable device made of two lengths of wood, which can be attached to a flat by a hook at the top and fixed to the floor with a stage screw or weight, for the purpose of keeping the scenery rigid. Also called a 'stage brace'. See 'French brace'.
BRAIL	A line used to pull and retain any piece of hanging scenery from its normal vertical position.
BUSINESS	Stage action as opposed to dialogue.
CARPET CUT	A narrow trap door immediately upstage of the house tabs which can be closed upon the downstage edge of a stage cloth to hold it in position.
CLEAT	A wooden or metal fitting about which a line may be passed or made fast.
CLOTH	Any hanging canvas scenery. See 'cut cloth', 'drop', 'stage cloth'.
COUNTERWEIGHT SYSTEM	A method of flying scenery similar to that described under 'Grid' but where adjustable weights are used for balancing and ease of operation.
CURTAIN LINE	An imaginary line which marks the position of the house tabs when closed (or lowered).
CURTAIN SET	A setting comprising mainly curtains.
CUT	Any long opening in the stage floor.
CUT CLOTH	A cloth which has a part cut away to show another cloth set behind. Often painted to represent trees or foliage, and sometimes the cut-away portion is filled with gauze.
CYCLORAMA	A plain curved backing to the stage; either a permanent structure or a stretched cloth used to represent the sky and giving an illusion of infinity.
DEAD	(*a*) A term used when a border or a suspended piece of scenery is at its correct position in the setting.
	(*b*) A term used when a piece of scenery or property is no longer required. The converse is to 'keep alive'.
DIM	A direction to check or decrease the intensity of light on the stage.
DIPS	Small traps in the floor of the stage containing plug sockets for electrical units.
DOOR FLAT	A flat into which a door unit has been fitted.
DOOR UNIT	Practical door in a wooden frame that can be fitted into a flat.
DRAPES	Any fabric hanging in folds as a scene, or part of a scene. Also casements and window curtains.
DRAW TABS	Curtains which open by being drawn to the sides.
DROP-CURTAIN	See 'act drop'.
FALSE PROSCENIUM	A structure or arrangement or scenery immediately behind the proscenium arch to lessen the height and width of the stage. Called 'Show portal' in America.
FESTOON TABS	A curtain with several lines passing through rings sewn to webbing on the upstage side, which when raised hangs in swags.
FIRE CURTAIN	See 'safety curtain'.
FLAT	A unit section of flat scenery constructed of canvas stretched on a tall wooden frame.

FLIES	(Fly, floor or flying gallery). The narrow gallery some distance above the stage and extending along a side wall of the stage from whence the ropes used to fly the scenery are operated.
FLIPPER	A small piece of flat scenery hinged to a larger flat.
FLOATS	The footlights. Used to counteract the shadows cast by overhead lighting. Frequently dispensed with in modern productions. The name is supposed to derive from the time when the forestage was illuminated by wicks floating in oil.
FLOWN	Suspended on lines from the grid.
FLYMAN	Stage hand employed in the flies.
F.O.H.	Front of House—the vestibules and foyer of the theatre. Also used to describe the lanterns in the auditorium that are used to illuminate the stage.
FORE STAGE	See 'apron'.
FRENCH BRACE	Triangular wooden frame, hinged to the back of a piece of standing scenery and, weighted, used to support it. It can be folded flat for storage.
FRENCH FLAT	Several flats, battened together, and flown as a unit.
GAUZE	Fine netting or similar material. It can be painted. When lit from the front only, it appears opaque and any painted decoration is revealed. When lit only from behind, it becomes transparent. It is useful for transformation and 'flash back' scenes.
GRID	A network of steel and/or wooden beams, high above the stage, used to support the lines used to fly the scenery, lighting battens and drapes.
GROUND PLAN	Scale plan of the stage (often $\frac{1}{2}$ inch to 1 foot), showing the position of the scenery in a setting.
GROUND ROW	Low piece of flat scenery, often with a profiled edge, painted and free standing. Usually represents a distant mountain range or a grassy bank.
HOUSE TABS	The main curtains between the stage and the auditorium.
INSET	A small scene set within a larger one.
IRON	See 'safety curtain'.
JOG	Narrow flat used as a small return to give the illusion of solidity.
LEG	A length of canvas or material used as a wing. Curtain sets are made up of tabs, legs and borders.
LINES (*Set of*)	The unit group of suspension lines hanging from the grid and used for flying the scenery. Usually three to a set, and known as short, centre and long line, reading from the fly gallery.
LONGARM	A long piece of wood used to free scenery or lines which may have accidentally fouled or caught up. Also called a clearing stick.
MASKING	A piece of scenery, not necessarily painted, used to obscure from the audience any part of the stage that should not be seen. Returns and backings are forms of masking.
OFFSTAGE	Any portion of the stage outside the audience's field of vision.
ON STAGE	Any part of the stage within the acting area.
OP (*Opposite Prompt*)	Stage right from the actor's point of view. If the prompt corner is situated here, it is sometimes called 'bastard prompt'.
PACK	A stack of flats used in a given scene and their correct order for setting.
PERMANENT MASKING	The false proscenium, or the teaser and tormentors or a similar arrangement of masking pieces, which remain in position throughout the performance.
PIN HINGE	A hinge with a removable pin so that the two halves can be easily separated.
PORTAL	An American term for the proscenium arch.
PRACTICAL	Capable of being used for its apparent function, e.g. an actual window as opposed to a painted one.
PRIMING	A solution of whiting and size used as a primer in scene painting.
PROMPT SIDE (PS)	Stage left from the actor's point of view, irrespective of the position of the prompter.
PROPERTIES (PROPS)	All objects used on the stage that cannot be regarded as costumes or scenery.
PROSCENIUM (PROS)	Comprises the proscenium opening and its surrounding treatment. Theoretically the 'fourth wall' of the stage.
PROSCENIUM OPENING OR ARCH	The opening through which the audience view the stage.

RAMP	An inclined rostrum.
RETURN	Flat leading 'off' at a right-angle to another.
REVEAL	A piece of timber or other material fixed to the edge of an opening to give the impression of thickness.
ROSTRUM	A platform. Small rostrums are usually rigid, but larger ones are made up of collapsible frames and a loose top which slots into position.
SAFETY CURTAIN	A fire-resistant shutter or curtain mounted immediately behind the proscenium arch. Usually made of a steel framework faced with iron or asbestos. It has a quick release device to enable it to be lowered speedily in the event of a fire on the stage.
SANDBAG	A sand-filled canvas bag, having a large ring, used for weighting purposes.
SET PIECE	A built-up unit of free-standing scenery, often three dimensional.
SETTING LINE	An imaginary line across the front of the stage, below which no scenery may be set.
SILL IRON	A thin strip of metal used to brace the bottom opening of a door flat or arch.
SKYCLOTH	A back cloth painted to represent the sky.
SPOTLINE	A single line specially rigged from the grid to fly a piece of scenery or property. Chandeliers are often flown on a spotline.
STAGECLOTH	A large piece of canvas used to cover the floor of the stage and often painted to represent marble, paving, grass, etc.
STAGESCREW	A large tapered screw with a handle, used to secure a stage brace to the stage instead of using a stageweight or sandbag.
STAGEWEIGHT	Large shaped iron weight which fits over the bottom fitment of a stage brace, to secure it steady.
STILE	The upright member in the framework of a flat.
STRIKE	Take apart and remove a set.
TEASER	A border hung between the tormentors.
THROWLINE	A length of cord attached to a flat and used to secure it to an adjacent flat.
THROWLINE CLEAT	A metal fitting around which the throwline is passed when securing adjacent pieces together.
TIE-OFF CLEAT	The metal fitting around which a throwline is made fast.
TORMENTOR	A permanent wing, immediately upstage of the proscenium arch, used to mask the offstage edges of the setting. Can be part of the false proscenium.
TRAILERS	See 'draw tabs'.
TRIM	To level off a piece of suspended scenery at the right height. Once trimmed it can be 'deaded'.
TRIP	To raise a piece of flown scenery using extra lines at the bottom edge, so that it can occupy approximately half its height. Used when there is insufficient stage height to fly away the piece normally.
TUMBLER	A roller fixed to the bottom edge of a cloth so that the cloth can be rolled up when not in use.
WING	The off-stage spaces or the OP and PS.
WING SET	A set comprising backcloth, wings and borders. Usually an exterior scene and used extensively in musical productions.

Bibliography

ACTING AND PRODUCTION TECHNIQUES

Albright, Halstead and Mitchell	Principles of Theatre Art	Houghton Miflin Co. 1955
Battye, Marguerite	Stage Movement	Herbert Jenkins 1954
Blakelock, Denys	Making the Stage your Career	Foyle 1965
Blakelock, Denys	Acting My Way	Favil Press 1965
Boleslavsky, Richard	Acting; The first six lessons	Dennis Dobson 1966
Bradbury and Howard	Stagecraft	Herbert Jenkins 1957
Butler, Ivan	Producing Pantomime and Revue	Foyle 1962
Canfield, Curtis	The Craft of Play Directing	Holt, Rinehart and Winston Inc. 1963
Coffin, L. Charteris	Stage Speech	Herbert Jenkins 1963
Dean, Alexander	Fundamentals of Play Directing	Holt, Rinehart and Winston Inc. 1965
*Dolman, Jr., John	The Art of Acting	Harper and Row 1949
*Dolman, Jr., John	The Art of Play Production	Harper and Row 1928
Fernald, John	The Play Produced	Deane 1933
Fishman, Morris	The Actor in Training	Herbert Jenkins 1961
Fishman, Morris	Play Production; Methods and Practice	Herbert Jenkins 1965
Gassner, John	Producing the Play	Holt, Rinehart and Winston Inc. 1965
Heffner, Selden and Sellman	Modern Theatre Practice	Vision 1961
Lamb, Frank	Producing a Play	Foyle 1954
Mackenzie, Frances	Approach to Theatre (for Student Producers)	Samuel French 1957
Mackenzie, Frances	The Amateur Actor; A Theatre Handbook	Garnet Miller 1966
Mackinlay, Leila	Musical Productions	Herbert Jenkins 1955
Marshall, Norman	The Producer and the Play	Macdonald 1962
Melvill, Harald	Theatrecraft	Rockliff 1954
Melvill, Harald	Complete Guide to Amateur Dramatics	Barrie and Rockliff 1962
Oxenford, Lyn	Playing Period Plays	Garnet Miller 1966
Oxenford, Lyn	Design for Movement	Garnet Miller 1964
*Purdom, C. B.	Producing Plays	J. M. Dent 1951
Richmond, Susan	A Textbook of Stagecraft	Deane 1932
Seyler, Athene and Haggard Stephen	The Craft of Comedy	Garnet Miller 1958
*Smethurst, Harold	Opera Production for Amateurs	Turnstile Press 1951
Stanislavski, Constantin	Creating a Role	Bles 1963
Stanislavski, Constantin	An Actor Prepares	Bles 1937, Penguin 1967
Stanislavski, Constantin	Building a Character	Max Reinhardt 1950
Turfery and Palmer	The Musical Production	Pitman 1953
Wykes, Alan	The Pan Book of Amateur Dramatics	Pan Books 1965
White, Edwin C.	Acting (Practical Stage Handbook)	Herbert Jenkins 1960

MUSIC, SINGING AND CONDUCTING

Aiken, W. A.	The Voice	Longmans 1963
*Bowles, Michael	The Art of Conducting	Doubleday and Co., Inc. 1959
Cox-Ife, William	The Elements of Conducting	John Barker 1964
Fuchs, Viktor	The Art of Singing and Voice Technique	John Calder 1963
*Graves, Richard M.	Singing for Amateurs	Oxford 1955
Lehmann, Lilli	How to Sing	Macmillan 1964
*Punt, Norman A.	The Singer's and Actor's Throat	Heinemann 1952
Rose, Arnold	The Singer and the Voice	Faber and Faber 1962

SPEECH

Aikin, W. A.	*The Voice*	Longmans 1963
Cole, Wilton	*Sound and Sense*	Allen and Unwin 1964
Colson, Greta	*Voice Production and Speech*	Museum Press 1963
Johnson, Harry	*Practical Speech Training*	Herbert Jenkins 1958
Marash, J. G.	*Effective Speaking*	Harrap 1964
Miles-Brown, J.	*Speech Training and Dramatic Art*	Pitman 1963
Parkin, K.	*Ideal Voice and Speech Training*	Samuel French 1962
Ridley, Frank	*A Manual of Elocution for Teacher and Student*	Samuel French 1928
Thurburn, G.	*Voice and Speech*	Nisbet 1965
Turner, J. Clifford	*Voice and Speech in the Theatre*	Pitman 1966

STAGE MANAGEMENT

Cornberg and Gebauer	*A Stage-crew Handbook*	Harper and Row 1957
Goffin, Peter	*Stage Management*	J. Garnet Miller 1963
Melvill, Harald	*Stage Management in the Amateur Theatre*	Barrie and Rockliff 1963

PROPERTIES

Conway, Heather	*Stage Properties*	Herbert Jenkins 1959
Kenton, Warren	*Stage Properties and How to Make Them*	Pitman 1966
Macnamara, Desmond	*A New Art of Papier Maché*	Arco 1963
Slade, Richard	*Masks and how to make them*	Faber and Faber 1964

EFFECTS

Green, Michael	*Stage Noises and Effects*	Herbert Jenkins 1958
Napier, Frank	*Noises Off*	J. Garnet Miller 1962

SCENIC CONSTRUCTION AND PAINTING

Adix, Vern	*Theatre Scenecraft*	Children's Theatre Press 1956
Bradbury, A. J. and Howard, W. R. B.	*Stagecraft*	Herbert Jenkins 1957
Buerki, F. A.	*Stagecraft for non-professionals*	University of Wisconsin Press 1962
Burris-Meyer and Cole	*Scenery for the Theatre*	Little, Brown and Co. 1938
*Carrick, Edward	*Designing for Films*	Studio Publications 1949
Friederich and Fraser	*Scenery Design for the Amateur Stage*	Macmillan 1964
Gillette, A. S.	*Stage Scenery, its construction and rigging*	Harper and Row 1959
Joseph, Stephen	*Scene Painting and Design*	Pitman 1964
Melvill, Harald	*Designing and Painting Scenery for the Theatre*	Barrie and Rockliff 1963
Parker and Smith	*Scene Design and Stage Lighting*	Holt, Rinehart and Winston Inc. 1963
Southern, Richard	*Proscenium and Sight-lines*	Faber and Faber 1964
Southern, Richard	*Stage-setting for Amateurs and Professionals*	Faber and Faber 1964
Warre, Michael	*Designing and Making Stage Scenery*	Studio Vista 1966
Wyatt, Jenifer	*Stage Scenery*	Herbert Jenkins 1957

LIGHTING

*Bentham, Frederick	*Stage Lighting*	Pitman 1968
Corry, P.	*Lighting the Stage*	Pitman 1964
Fuchs, Theodore	*Stage Lighting*	Benjamin Bloom 1963
Goffin, Peter	*Stage Lighting for Amateurs*	J. Garnet Miller 1952
Ost, Geoffrey	*Stage Lighting*	Herbert Jenkins 1957
Parker and Smith	*Scene Design and Stage Lighting*	Holt, Rinehart and Winston Inc. 1963
Rubin and Watson	*Theatrical Lighting Practice*	Theatre Arts Books 1954
Say, M. G.	*Lighting the Amateur Stage*	Albyn Press 1956

COSTUME

Arnold, Janet	*Patterns of Fashion, Englishwomen's Dresses and Their Construction, c. 1660–1860*	Wace 1964
Arnold, Janet	*Patterns of Fashion, Englishwomen's Dresses and Their Construction, c. 1860–1940*	Wace 1966
Barton, Lucy	*Historic Costume for the Stage*	A. and C. Black 1961
Bradley, Carolyn	*A History of World Costume*	Peter Owen 1964
Clarke, Joan	*English Costume Through The Ages*	E.U.P. 1966
Cunnington and Beard	*A Dictionary of English Costume*	A. and C. Black 1960
Fernald and Shenton	*Costume Design and Making*	A. and C. Black 1967
Green, Ruth M.	*The Wearing of Costume*	Pitman 1966
Hansen, Henny H.	*Costume Cavalcade*	Methuen 1964
Laver, James (introduced by)	*Costume through the Ages*	Thames and Hudson 1964
Lister, Margot	*Stage Costume*	Herbert Jenkins 1961
Mann, Kathleen	*Peasant Costume in Europe*	A. and C. Black 1961
Melvill, Harald	*Historic Costume for the Amateur Stage*	Barrie and Rockliff 1961
Motley	*Designing and Making Stage Costumes*	Studio Vista 1964
Paterek, Josephine D.	*Costuming for the Theatre*	Crown Publications 1959
Truman, Nevil	*Historic Costuming*	Pitman 1966
Walkup, Fairfax Proudfit	*Dressing the Part*	Peter Owen 1962
White, A. V.	*Making Stage Costumes for Amateurs*	Routledge and Kegan Paul 1963
Yarwood, Doreen	*English Costume*	Batsford 1964

MAKE-UP

Asser, Joyce	*Historic Hairdressing*	Pitman 1966
Bamford, T. W.	*Practical Make-up for the Stage*	Pitman 1940
Benoliel, M. H.	*Stage Make-up Made Easy*	Deane 1946
Blore, Richard (of Leichner)	*Stage Make-up*	Stacey Publications 1965
Corson, Richard	*Stage Make-up*	Peter Owen 1967
Emerald, Jack	*Make-up in Amateur Movies, Drama and Photography*	Fountain Press 1966
Kehoe, Vincent, J. R.	*The Technique of Film and Television Make-up*	Focal Press 1966
Liszt, Dr. Rudolph G.	*The Last Word in Make-up*	Dramatist's Play Service 1964
Melvill, Harald	*Magic of Make-up*	Barrie and Rockliff 1965
Mill, Callum	*Make-up for the Amateur*	Albyn Press 1955
Perrottet, Phillippe	*Practical Stage Make-up*	Studio Vista 1967
Sequeira, Horace	*Stage Make-up*	Herbert Jenkins 1957
Stanley, Adrian	*A Guide to Greasepaint*	Samuel French 1953
Ward, Eric	*A Book of Make-up*	Samuel French 1930

GENERAL REFERENCE

Baily, Leslie	*The Gilbert and Sullivan Book*	Cassell and Co. Ltd 1956
Chisman and Raven-Hart	*Manners and Movements in Costume Plays*	Deane 1934
*Downs, Harold (edited by)	*Theatre and Stage*, two vols.	Pitman 1935
Ewen, David	*The Story of America's Musical Theatre*	Chilton Co. 1961
Gaye, Freda (edited by)	*Who's Who in the Theatre* (14th edit.)	Pitman 1967
Hartnoll, Phyllis (edited by)	*Oxford Companion to the Theatre*	Oxford 1967
Hobbs, William	*Techniques of the Stage Fight*	Studio Vista 1967
Lubbock, Mark	*The Complete Book of Light Opera*	Pitman 1962
McSpadden, J. Walker	*Opera Synopses*	Harrap 1949
Moore, Frank L.	*The Handbook of Gilbert and Sullivan*	Arthur Barker 1962
Oxenford, Lyn	*Playing Period Plays*	Garnet Miller 1966
Stacey, Roy	*Theatrical Directory*	Stacey Publications 1967
Suddards and White	*The Law and the Amateur Theatre*	Samuel French 1962

| Wildeblood and Brinson | *The Polite World* | Oxford University Press 1966 |
| Williamson, Audrey | *Gilbert and Sullivan Opera* | Rockliff 1955 |

* The books marked thus are out of print, but should be available from good reference libraries.

USEFUL PERIODICALS

Amateur Stage	Stacey Publications	Published monthly 2s. 6d.
Dance and Dancers	Seven Arts Group	Published monthly 3s.
The Dancing Times	The Dancing Times	Published monthly 3s.
Drama	British Drama League	Published quarterly 2s.
Musical Opinion	Musical Opinion Ltd	Published monthly 2s.
Noda Bulletin	National Operatic and Drama Association	Published three times a year—free to members
Opera	Rolls House Publishing Co. Ltd	Published monthly
Plays and Players	Seven Arts Group	Published monthly 4s.
The Stage	Carson and Comerford Ltd	Published weekly 9d.
Tabs	Strand Electric and Engineering Co. Ltd	Published three times a year—free on request
Theatre Notebook	22 Buckingham Gate, S.W.1.	Published quarterly

ORGANIZATIONS INTERESTED IN THE AMATEUR THEATRE MOVEMENT

Arts Council of Great Britain, 4 St. James's Square, London, S.W.1.
British Council, 65 Davies Street, London, W.1.
British Drama League, 9 Fitzroy Square, London, W.1.
International Theatre Institute, British Centre, 22 Duchy Street, London, S.E.1.
League of Dramatists, 81 Drayton Gardens, London, S.W.10.
National Operatic and Dramatic Association, 1 Crestfield Street, London, W.C.1.

Index